From Autopilot ^{to}Authentic

How the Philosophies of Dr. Tom Hill Can Help You Live Your Exceptional Life

BRETT A. BLAIR

Foreword

"Dad, will you co-sign on Brett's new car?" my daughter Michelle asked one afternoon in the spring of 1983.

Michelle was a student at the University of Missouri, where I was also working as the director of the state's 4-H system. Her boyfriend, Brett Blair, had just graduated with an industrial engineering degree at the same university, and was working at the nearby 3M plant in Columbia, Missouri. As with most American boys after landing their first big job, he wanted to buy a new car. Finding a speedy red Pontiac Fiero, but having no credit history, he needed someone to co-sign his car loan.

"Yes," I said. "He's a fine young man."

Over the past 32 years, Brett Blair and I have crossed paths several times on the beautiful tapestry called life. Brett went on to obtain his MBA, and enjoyed a very successful career at Alcoa. Marrying young, (but not to my daughter Michelle), Brett raised a wonderful family of three children, and had what appeared to be the perfect life.

Twenty-three years later, in the fall of 2006, something inside of Brett was stirring, and he knew things were not quite right. He was living a good life, but was it his right life? He was outwardly successful, but was he making a difference? He had a great marriage, a wonderful family, a growing career with money and security, good health and good friends. What more could he want? Feeling somewhat guilty about secretly wanting more, he recognized that his life felt like he was on a treadmill, going faster and faster, but going nowhere at all. He couldn't connect his work to anything real or meaningful. His career began to feel like a crazy game.

Over the next eight years, Brett's life went through a remarkable set of challenges, awakenings, heartbreak, excitement and joy. After leaving Alcoa to start his own executive recruiting firm in 2007, Brett reached out to me to be his life coach. Brett recognized that there was much more to life than what he had been experiencing, and that he wanted coaching to help guide and propel his growth. At that point in time, I had sold my interests in my RE/MAX businesses, and was devoting myself full time to coaching and speaking. Brett and I quickly became close friends, and he proved to be a uniquely disciplined student of the concepts and philosophies of life that I shared with him.

Brett is now giving back. In addition to rigorously applying the concepts I have taught him, Brett is also a graduate of the Arête High Performance Advisor training program. A voracious reader and learner, Brett has studied and applied, in his own life, the principles of success from dozens of other authors and proven professionals.

Brett and I have a common story, in that we both left the comfort and security of our prior careers to embark upon an uncertain future. I was blessed to find great success and happiness in my years with RE/MAX and beyond. Brett is similarly successful in his second career as the owner of Sanford Rose Associates–Brighton Executive Search, as well as in his life coaching business, Blair Leadership Group. Brett continues to apply in his own life the principles of success described in this book. He has a huge appetite for growth and balance, knowing that his future is limited only by his health and imagination.

Brett's true purpose is helping other people. Openly sharing intimate details of his life, Brett wants to provide you, the reader, with an engaging, heartfelt story, with emotion and passion, as well as practical advice that can be applied in your own life. Hoping to help other people figure out their own true passions, and to become unstuck and get on the path to achieving their unique dreams—that is the real purpose for this book.

You will find this book, *From Autopilot to Authentic*, to be an emotional roller coaster that will pull you in and speak to your heart. Everyone can relate to elements of Brett's life and story, and his unique message will provide you with the insights, advice and inspiration to go forth and design and live your own exceptional life.

Dr. Tom Hill

Contents

*To my mentor, my life coach, and my
very good friend, Dr. Tom Hill*

"Most men lead lives of quiet desperation and go to the grave with their song still in them."

~HENRY DAVID THOREAU

Introduction: Why I wrote this book

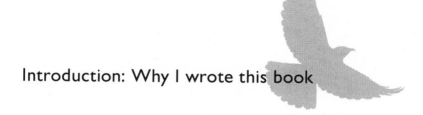

This is a book about hope. This is a book about change. This is a book about the opportunity that we all have to design our own lives and pursue a beautiful future, regardless of our age or situation in life.

At 45 years of age, I had a mid-life thing happen to me. Some people have mid-life crises. Others have mid-life tragedies. Many have mid-life stagnation, boredom, or sadness. The lucky ones go through the mid-life years well, continuing on their correct, chosen path. As for me, on the outside, my life was great. I had good health, a good marriage, great kids and a great job. My career was progressing well, and other than the usual bumps along the road at work and at home, all was peachy. The problem: I was on autopilot. I didn't know what I didn't know, and was living a life according to other people's expectations. I wasn't living the life that was authentic for me, and I had no idea. Thank God I experienced some events along the way that woke me up. Through synchronicity, mentoring, tragedy and therapy, I came to recognize the wrong path that I was on, and the wrong habits and ways of thinking that were holding me back.

Tom Hill, my long-time mentor and life coach, has been a central figure in the growth and trajectory of my life, and this book is dedicated to him and his family. I am forever blessed to have crossed paths with Tom, from my college years when he was an administrator with the University of Missouri, to our time working together in selling RE/MAX franchises, to his ongoing dedication to me and my family as my life coach and friend over the past decade. Tom has taught me the simple, profound and timeless principles from which to design and live out an exceptional life, and I pinch myself every day for the blessings that have come my way as a result.

> " No one should 'should' on their dreams. "

So why do I write this book? For two reasons:

One—to honor Tom Hill and the impact he has had on me and thousands of others around the world who have benefited from his speaking, writing, coaching, mentoring, and friendship.

Two—to inspire you, the reader, to take an honest look at your own life, and to provide you the encouragement to take action—so you will move toward your authentic self. My hope is that this book will provide you with the principles and practical advice for moving forward and achieving your unique dreams. Remember, no one should "should" on their dreams!

Chapter One: The Treadmill

Drip—drip—drip.

What's that noise? My eyes snap open. Where am I? Oh, yeah—I'm in Las Vegas. This room, it's so dark—and it smells of cigarettes and Lysol. I squint toward the alarm clock—4:30 a.m. Carol's sound asleep next to me.

Drip—drip—drip.

I get up and go to the bathroom. That rusty faucet is leaking, and it won't stop. We're here to celebrate our daughter Dana's 21st birthday, and she and her friend are in the other room in our suite. "Suite?" I don't think so! This is what we get for trying to land a bigger room without spending any money. What a dump!

That feeling washes back over me again—the one I'm used to pretty much every morning these past few months. I wish I were dreaming, but I know I'm not. I'm fully awake, in a life that feels like a nightmare.

I move to the desk, and quietly open up my laptop. I'm sleepy, exhausted, and full of dread. The pressure at work has been relentless, and almost unbearable. Cooling fan controllers are failing every day, and no one is there to help. As the general manager of our electronics division, fixing this problem is all mine. Bob Rodgers and Frank Smith are both demanding solutions while not offering any help. I used to like those guys, and thought they would be better than this. The conference calls with General Motors and Continental are becoming intense. The guys in Mexico making these parts are over their heads, and they're faking it. Cars are catching on fire. Thank God there hasn't been a wreck or someone killed. I worry and wonder if there will be a recall. If that happens— what will happen to me? What will happen to the company? What am I doing? I feel so disconnected. I feel lost.

Not too long ago, I read a little book called *The Prayer of Jabez*. I don't read much—maybe a book a year—but this is a tiny little book. I've been leading the high school youth group at All Saints Lutheran Church, and thought this may be a good book to help me become more qualified. I love those high school kids, but I'm not sure I'm the right one to be leading a youth group. The prayer described in this book hit me. I changed it up a bit, adding it to a prayer that I had crafted 25 years earlier, during the process to become an Eagle Scout.

That original Eagle Scout version went something like this:

Dear God. Please forgive me of my sins. Please help me to become a better person. Please help me to be strong and happy. In Jesus Christ's name I pray.

I added ...

Dear God, please bless me. Bless me in ways I can't imagine. It is through your blessings to me that I can be able to help and bless other people.

Please add to my territory—by growing my network each and every day. I want to touch and help more and more people.

Please lift me up as you ask me to do big things—things that I have never done before.

Please keep me from evil—from sin.

Then, I added a prayer of thanksgiving.

Dear God—thank you. Thank you for all of my countless blessings. I love you. Amen.

I quietly say the prayer, mouthing the words at barely a whisper. Carol is still asleep. Over the past few months I've made it a habit to wake up with this prayer, and it seems especially appropriate right now, being in Vegas and all.

As I finish saying the prayer, it hits me again. I've been wondering about something. I'm such a hypocrite. Do I really mean what I'm saying? If I do, I'm living a life of contradiction. I'm

> 66 I feel like I'm on a treadmill, going faster and faster, and going absolutely nowhere. 99

sure as hell not meeting new people these days or "expanding my territory." In fact, my little life is getting smaller and smaller and more inwardly focused.

I get up early every morning, drive to the office, sit in my cubicle and stare at my laptop. I answer the phone and emails and go to meetings, then drive home, be with the family, go to bed, get up, go back to the office, and do it all over again. I feel like I'm on a treadmill, going faster and faster and faster, and going absolutely nowhere. I'm 45, married with three great kids. A good job, nice salary, stock options, big house and a boat and cars. Five dogs. Church, vacations, pension, security. Friends? Not all that many and none very close. Extended family? All in different parts of the country. Work? Work is becoming this crazy game. All pretend and BS. Predict the division's sales and profits for the coming month, quarter and year—and make PowerPoint slides to present to senior leaders. This takes a couple of weeks. Then when we miss the sales and profit projections, I make PowerPoint slides to explain the miss and what will be done to correct it—again, with more promises. This takes another couple of weeks. All month long is a vicious cycle of promises and explaining. In the meantime, I get paid really well. The exact same amount every two weeks. Also, by playing the game right, there'll be a big bonus in March, and if the parent company's stock price happens to go up, an even bigger payout by cashing in stock options. Big money if the stock goes up. Zero money if the stock goes down. My

> 66 On autopilot heading to who knows where. 99

work has absolutely no impact on which direction it goes. Feels kind of like Vegas. Wait—I'm in Vegas. And I don't even like to gamble. That familiar dread settles back in as I snap to the reality of the mounting quality problems at work. This sucks.

I don't feel connected to anything real in my job. It's just a big game. I'm surrounded by pretenders. What has happened to me? What has happened to my life? I feel sick—in my stomach and in my heart. Lost. Alone. On autopilot heading to who knows where. It sure feels like a very dark place.

The computer screen lights up. I connect to the hotel wireless, and go to Outlook. Email messages pop in, one by one. Quality problem. Mandatory meeting. Profit miss. Quality problem. Quality problem. Vehicle fire report. Quality issues meeting invitation.

Tom Hill's Friday Eaglezine

Tom Hill? Hmmm … how long has it been? I wonder what he's been up to.

* * *

When I was a kid, I used to love to read encyclopedias. I would sneak away and spend hours absorbing every page. I dreamed of inventing something really big that would somehow change the world. I wanted to write a novel. I wanted to run my own business. I wanted to be a millionaire by the time I turned thirty. I was the dutiful son, the oldest of three kids. I always followed the rules, while my younger brother Mark was always getting in trouble. Mark and Tracey are twins, born just thirteen months after me to our very, very young parents. Most people thought that Tracey and I should have been the twins. She was also a dutiful rule follower.

I loved Boy Scouts and especially camping every month. I hung in there and got my Eagle Scout award just before I turned sixteen. Good thing—because my car and new focus on girls would have ended all that. I was a little guy—98 pounds as a freshman. One hundred twenty-six pounds as a senior. I lettered every year in wrestling, even as a freshman. This was the first time I felt proud at school. I ran cross-country to get in shape for wrestling. I hated running, but was proud of the conditioning and how much I was in better shape when wrestling season came around. Girls started to be attracted to me. I drove a 1963 Chevy Impala convertible, black with a white top, and worked at the Dairy Queen and then at Blue Springs Bank as a teller. I learned that I loved working with people. With wheels and some money, I had a couple of serious girlfriends, but absolutely no sex. I wouldn't do it. My sophomore year girlfriend broke up with me because I wouldn't do it. She said it showed how little I cared for her. I was scared to death of sex after watching my 17-year-old friend get pregnant and drop out of high school.

I was one of two kids nominated from our high school to go to Missouri Boy's State, a weeklong camp to learn about politics and participate in mock elections and government. My wrestling coach and the school principal saw something in me that I didn't see in myself. This would be a recurring theme in my life.

When it became time to choose a college and a degree, I had no idea what I wanted to do. I was the first to go to college on both sides of the family, and although my parents pushed all three of us kids to get good grades and go on to college, they didn't save any money for it, nor was there any help on how to go about it. They were doing all they could do to pay the bills.

Following the crowd from my high school, I applied to the University of Missouri (Mizzou) and got accepted. Without any idea at all about what I would do for a career, I went to the school counseling office and thumbed through the book of degrees and average salaries. It was clear that engineering was one of the highest paying degrees. I was not good at math or science, with zero interest in mechanical things. But I was interested in business, and I found an engineering degree called "Industrial Engineering," that looked like it was something about making factories more profitable. This degree didn't require nearly as much chemistry, physics and other sciences as the other engineering degrees, so I chose it. I was going to be an industrial engineer! I was awarded several small scholarships and paid for the rest of college through student loans.

When I told my parents that I was going to be an industrial engineer, my dad made fun of me. He said that industrial engineers are "chicken checkers." These were the guys that went out on the plant floor with a stopwatch and a clipboard to time-study the workers. Dad hated these guys, as a lot of his friends worked on the plant floor. He said that everyone hates these guys. He wanted me to go to Warrensburg and be a teacher. I knew that teachers didn't make much money.

I loved my dad and really looked up to him. As a young boy, I loved to go out fishing with him. We'd sit in the boat all night, fishing for crappie, and come back in as the sun was starting to rise. I felt like a man. Those were great times, but during college I started to see something different. I wondered if he was jealous of the money I would make. I knew that he would be proud, but it sure didn't feel that way.

I remembered going to the Kansas City Royals baseball game with my dad—and asking him what inning it was. He said, "The sixth."

"How do you know that?" I asked.

"Look at the scoreboard. There, just below the score."

I couldn't see it. I was eight years old and blind as a bat. I recalled taking an eye exam at school, and when I couldn't read even the big letters at the top, the nurse-lady told me to step out of the line. I guess they forgot to follow up with me. I was too shy to say anything. After getting my eyes examined and a pair of black-rimmed glasses, I rode home from the eye doctor on the back of my dad's motorcycle, holding him tight. As I looked up, I saw for the very first time in many years birds on the power lines. Then I watched one with my new visual clarity as it took off in flight. I felt a connection to that bird.

> I felt a connection to that bird.

I joined the Sigma Nu Fraternity and loved it. My parents divorced during my freshman year in college. When my brother Mark called to tell me this was the first and only time I ever heard him cry. I think that Tracey was actually relieved. She and Dad seemed to grow apart during her high school years.

After finishing my sophomore year at Mizzou, I was completely burnt out with school. I saw a poster stapled to a telephone pole advertising an exchange program in Japan. Japanese manufacturing was starting to be the rage, and I wondered if some time in Japan would help me in my engineering career. That was the official reason. I was really looking for an escape. Over several beers, two of my fraternity brothers and I dared each other to go for it. We all applied for the program and soon all three of us were formally accepted. My first time in an airplane was at twenty years old, flying from Kansas City to Los Angeles, then on to Tokyo. I attended Sophia University's International Campus in the Ichigaya section of Tokyo, and lived in a dorm with two other guys—one from Germany and one from Japan. I loved living and studying in Japan, and learned how to read and write Japanese.

At a Halloween party on campus, I met a beautiful girl, Yasuko, and we started dating immediately. I loved this girl, and we discretely made plans for her to return to Missouri with me after my exchange program ended. Her father was a very successful dentist, and he had a young dental student in mind for Yasuko as her future husband. She broke up with me over the Christmas holiday, while a large group of us students were snow skiing in northern Japan. That hurt. I was depressed until I returned home at the end of March.

College life at Mizzou improved, and the engineering curriculum became less intense. I matured quite a bit during my time in Japan, and I refined my study skills. Learning the Japanese language—especially reading and writing, forced me to study at a whole 'nother level.

I also started to quickly lose my hair. It just started falling out, in big clumps. It was devastating going bald at 21 years young. After getting teased and harassed by my buddies, and briefly trying some anti-balding scheme I saw advertised, I ultimately gave in to my fate. My mom's dad and both of her brothers were completely bald, so I knew I had the dreaded bald genes. Thankfully I never succumbed to the comb-over, and I recognized the blessing that I would never have a mid-life crisis for losing my hair. Also, I noticed that girls didn't seem to mind anyway.

After two more years at Mizzou and life at the Sigma Nu fraternity, I graduated with my industrial engineering degree. Just before my "final senior year," at Mizzou, I met Michelle. Michelle and I fell in love right away. She was a beautiful incoming freshman, and I was about to start my final year. I had a job as an intern engineer at the nearby 3M plant. Michelle grew up in Fulton, about a 30-minute drive from Columbia. Over the coming weeks I met her mom and stepdad in Fulton, and her dad and stepmom in Columbia. Michelle's dad was an administrator at the University of Missouri—Dr. Tom Hill. Tom and his wife Betty lived in Columbia with Betty's daughter, Nina. Tom was a great guy to have as your girlfriend's dad, and we got along very well. Tom even co-signed on my first new car loan, for a beautiful 1984 Pontiac Fiero.

Upon graduating with my industrial engineering degree, I was hired full-time at 3M as a process engineer. After a couple of years of dating Michelle she broke up with me on Valentine's Day, after our date. She told me that she wanted "space." I later learned that this was code for "met someone else." I was heartbroken for several months. My work at 3M was monotonous, and I was frustrated that they wouldn't let me travel or do projects in Japan. For the next year I lived in a small condominium that I bought in Columbia, worked at 3M and lifted weights with some friends, and casually dated several girls. I was bored to death.

Tom Hill called me one afternoon, many months after Michelle and I had broken up, and asked me to meet him at the Burger King for breakfast. I wondered what was up. Did I do something wrong? Was I in trouble? When I met up with Tom, he shared with me the excitement about his upcoming move to RE/MAX. He was going to resign from the University of Missouri, from a job which he could never be fired, and risk it all on a new concept in real estate franchise sales. I was enthralled by the idea, and immediately attracted to the dream that Tom shared. I felt my entrepreneurial urgings reignite, long dormant since early childhood. I decided that day to quit my job at 3M, and join Tom in selling RE/MAX franchises in South Georgia. After quickly selling my small condominium, I packed up my Pontiac Fiero and drove 1000 miles to Savannah, Georgia.

Working with Tom, I immediately started the prospecting and cold-call sales of the new RE/MAX real estate concept all across rural southern Georgia. I was 25, while most of my prospects were in their mid-50s or older. This didn't go well, to put it mildly. I had dreams of how much money I was going to make, and the real estate empire that I was going to build. Sales were tough to come by, and I was not showing much success. That is an understatement. I sucked. Tom was very supportive, but no matter how hard I tried, I just couldn't close the deals.

With RE/MAX I migrated north to Atlanta and stayed at the home of Tom's business partner, Howard. I went to class at night and obtained my Georgia real estate license. While attending class, I met a cute girl who seemed to have trouble with the material. I offered to help, and we met a couple of times at coffee shops to study. I asked where she worked, and she told me that she was a dancer. She invited me to come watch her performance. Mr. Naïve showed up again. I was not raised in a family of culture and the fine arts, so I didn't really know if I would like watching a ballet. When I arrived at her show, I quickly realized that I was confused. My friend was a stripper, and her "show" was at a men's club in the sleazy part of Atlanta. Luckily it was dark in there, or she would have seen how red my face was in embarrassment watching her take off her clothes. The next day in class she thanked me for dropping by her show, and we both went on with studying for the upcoming test. I passed the test. She did not, and I don't know what happened to her next. I grew up a bit.

In Atlanta, I found a 24/7 crazy buzz of activity, with traffic that I had never experienced. I attempted, again, mostly in vain, to sell RE/MAX real estate franchises all around town and the vast suburbs, which extended in all directions for miles and miles. After Tom and Howard purchased the RE/MAX rights for Kentucky and Tennessee, I then moved north again, this time to more laid back Louisville, Kentucky. Even though I was not making sales, I was enthusiastic about the future potential—especially of owning my own real estate company—and I recruited Chip Brandt, my previous Sigma Nu fraternity roommate, to join me in this venture. Chip courageously quit his job as an engineer at McDonnell Douglas in St. Louis, and he moved to Louisville, living with me in my apartment.

I met Carol on a blind date, set up by a RE/MAX franchise owner in Louisville. Carol was going through the final stages of her bitter divorce, and was ready to start dating. I was her first date post-divorce, and on our first meeting, I also met her sweet little girls, Ellen (five) and Dana (one). I soon fell in love with all three. Carol was four years older than me, but more like ten years older in life experience. She had already been married for eight years, and I was 25, a complete rookie in the marriage and family thing—feeling more like I was just out of the fraternity house.

Selling franchises continued to be very difficult. Carol and I grew closer. Chip made a smart move and went back to McDonnell Douglas. I couldn't pay all of my bills, and started missing student loan payments. I began to think about Carol for the long term. I met her parents and siblings—all great people. Her dad had previously retired from a very successful career with a broadcasting company. He entered his golden years with a comfortable nest egg and a pension. He was very gentle, humble, and wise. I grew to respect him and viewed him as a mentor. My entrepreneurial spirit was waning. I began to think that I may need to go out and get a "real job."

I interviewed for a quality manager position with a cardboard manufacturing company in Memphis. A very rough place in an even rougher part of town. Good thing I didn't get that job. I interviewed for a cost estimator position with a company called PEP Industries in Nashville, about three hours south of Louisville. This company was looking for an industrial engineer who spoke Japanese. "Hai!" ("Yes!" in Japanese). That was me! I interviewed in person, and was quickly offered the job at a salary of $26,500. I immediately said "yes," and moved to an apartment in nearby Bellevue. My boss was a non-stop coffee drinking, chain-smoking bundle of nerves, and I enjoyed working with many of the others who were all southerners. I learned some of the Nashville slang. "D'yanna co drank?" (Do you want a Coke?) "That's a fur piece from har." (That's pretty far away from here.)

I continued to see Carol on the weekends, usually driving back to Louisville. Sometimes she would drive to Nashville to visit me. I fell in love with Carol, Ellen and Dana. During this time I made several amazing trips to Japan with PEP Industries. Carol and the girls moved to Nashville in the summer. Carol was now officially divorced from Eric, who paid monthly child support. Eric had visitation rights to see the girls one weekend per month, and we would meet him halfway in Cave City, Kentucky.

We got married in November, 1987, at a nice little ceremony in Hilton Head, South Carolina, where Carol's parents lived most of the year. We drove Carol's Honda Civic station wagon, with both girls in the back seat, from Nashville to Hilton Head for the wedding. The day before the wedding, Ralph Jackson (Carol's dad) took me aside. He said, "Brett, you know that you don't have to go through with this." He told me that Carol was very strong willed, that there was a lot involved in raising kids, and that at my age, he wouldn't blame me if I chose not to get married. I replied, "Mr. Jackson, I love your daughter very much, and I intend to marry her." The night before the wedding, Carol got nervous and told me that she didn't think she could go through with it. She said that getting divorced the first time was too hard, and she didn't want to go through that pain again. My head was spinning. First her dad tells me that I could back out, and now Carol is getting cold feet. All of my family is in town, ready to celebrate, and I'm hearing this? I told Carol that if we didn't get married the next day, I would get on a plane and fly away to Japan and that she would never see me again. We got married the next day.

I received my MBA at Tennessee State University after two years of studying at night. During that period, Carol became pregnant but soon miscarried. Carol and her two sisters were in a casual race to see who would get pregnant first. Carol was now 33, and she was putting pressure on me to get her pregnant before her "body clock" expired. I thought it was interesting how young folks, often times not married and after one encounter, get pregnant, but it takes married folks sometimes years, if ever, to get pregnant. A few months later, as the time-pressure was building, Carol was pregnant again, and Patrick was born on April 9, 1990. Watching Patrick enter this world was a miracle for me, and I've loved being a parent for all three kids. Although I never adopted the girls, they treated me like their father, and all three kids called me Pop.

We soon bought a very nice house in the Cottonwood subdivision of Franklin, Tennessee. We were in a great neighborhood, with wonderful schools, friends, and activities. Carol purchased a home decorating franchise called Decorating Den, and she was great at helping people with color, upholstery and window treatments. Carol was proud that the business was profitable. We bought a small boat and enjoyed water skiing on weekends. I played soccer in an over-thirty league in the neighborhood, started running 5K's, and jumped into guitar lessons. We played golf with some friends and enjoyed going to church a couple of times per month.

PEP Industries was purchased by Alcoa, and became part of a joint venture called Alcoa Fujikura Limited (AFL). The business was growing like crazy. I moved up quickly in the company. On a three week business trip to Europe—which included time in Germany, the Czech Republic and Portugal, I was part of a team sent to evaluate a big potential acquisition. As a group we worked very hard, and on our last night in Lisbon, the entire group chose to celebrate. After too much food and wine, we all went back to our hotel to pack up and get some sleep before our long flight home the following day. My phone rang at 4 a.m. The hotel desk clerk asked me to come downstairs to the front office. My mind was spinning. What could this be about? When I entered the office, the hotel manager showed me my boss's U.S. Passport. He then explained that my boss had called complaining about chest pains, and they responded to his room immediately along with the paramedics, but they could not save him. My boss died of a massive heart attack.

> **I started, maybe for the first time, to ponder the real meaning of life.**

I quickly remembered his wife dropping us both off at the airport in Nashville three weeks prior, and watching my boss and wife kiss goodbye. I couldn't get that sight out of my mind. That was the last time she would ever see her husband alive. On the 10-hour flight home the following day, my head was spinning. I started, maybe for the first time, to ponder the real meaning of life.

In 1994, AFL's president decided to move the company's headquarters from Nashville to San Antonio, Texas. He wanted to be closer to the growing number of AFL manufacturing facilities in Mexico, and he wanted his key leadership team to be there as well. Carol agreed to the move, and we quickly sold our beloved home in Cottonwood. Carol also sold her Decorating Den van and closed her business. We bought a new two-story brick home in a growing subdivision in the sprawl of north San Antonio. Our backdoor neighbors, without our prior knowledge, were an AFL coworker and his wife, who also moved from Nashville. We bought a new red Ford Windstar minivan, and were set for our new suburban life in San Antonio.

When we arrived at our house on the scheduled move-in date, we found the house not quite ready. The carpet had not been laid, and there was still some painting and trim work to complete. We needed to spend a few days in a hotel, with our family of five and a dog. I saw something new in Carol. She snapped—showing intense, uncharacteristic anger at the builder for the inconvenience of the home not being ready. San Antonio was relentlessly hot and dry. Flat. Brown. Very few trees and those that were there were crippled-looking. We found scorpions in the new house, sometimes falling out of the air conditioning vents overhead. Carol started experiencing "crashes." These crashes were episodes of an unexplainable temporary paralysis.

My job was intense, and the stress very high. The career was progressing well, and I was soon moved into a human resources leadership role. With regular business travel to Mexico, I became fluent in Spanish, working with a tutor from Berlitz, a language training company.

In the years 1995 – 1996 – 1997, Carol's health continued to decline. The crashes happened more frequently, with increasing severity. With three young and very active kids, and a partially disabled wife, I was burning the candle at both ends. The stress level was high. For a while we had a live-in nanny. We bought a nicer, bigger boat. We joined the Sonterra Country Club. We pretended to have a happy, healthy life on the outside, but in the privacy of our home, Carol's health issues were anything but healthy. After two years in the new two-story house, Carol decided that we needed to move to a one-story, ranch-style home. We soon contracted to build a beautiful new home, with an in-ground pool, about five miles north, in what's called the Hill Country. We couldn't sell the first house, and it took about six months of making double house payments before we finally sold it at a huge loss. Poof ... I saw how fast money could disappear.

Patrick in elementary school, Dana in middle school, and Ellen in high school. All three kids thrived in their lives in San Antonio. My work continued to be fast-paced and stressful, but engaging. Carol continued to struggle with her health, and relied more and more on holistic remedies.

In early 2000, Carol told me that we needed to move back to Nashville. There was no sign that her health would improve, she hated living in San Antonio, and she simply wanted to be "back home." We had consulted with doctor after doctor, and no one could diagnose Carol's illness. Most doctors inferred that her health issues were stress-related, and she was prescribed various drugs, none of which seemed to help. After being diagnosed with fibromyalgia and chronic fatigue syndrome, neither of which has a cure, she met with one doctor who suggested that she may have cystic fibrosis. Upon hearing these words, and thinking that she would continue to decline, Carol wanted to be back in Tennessee. Being the dutiful follower husband that I was, I said okay, and I soon met with my boss and told him that I needed to resign. Upon learning more about Carol's health issues, my boss told me that I could not resign, but that instead I would be transferred to the company's new corporate office in Brentwood, a suburb of Nashville. Ellen graduated from high school, and went on to college at Texas A&M.

Carol, Dana, Patrick and I moved to an older ranch-style home in Brentwood. I was promoted to director of human resources, and was also put in charge of the project to locate and manage the move of our corporate office. We learned that Carol did not have cystic fibrosis, which was a huge relief.

Not long after, I was promoted to a position in business development, which required a lot of travel to Detroit. I had always wanted to move into a business leadership position with accountability for profit and loss. The company's president offered this career path to me on one condition— that I would move to the Detroit area. The travel from Nashville soon became too much, and Carol and I decided that it would be best if the family went ahead and moved to Detroit. Thankfully, the local real estate market was strong, and we quickly sold the house in Brentwood as we purchased and moved to a beautiful home in Brighton, Michigan. This house had a phenomenal backyard with an in-ground pool and adjacent pool house. Patrick attended Hartland Middle School, and Dana was a senior at Hartland High School. She was a real trooper about moving to a new school for her senior year. Winter hit hard, and we all learned what it was like to drive in snow every day.

As Patrick was approaching his 15th birthday, we bought him a 1999 Mustang GT. He was making good grades, and we wanted to encourage his progress. Dana graduated from Hartland High School, and went on to college at Auburn University in Alabama. She joined a sorority and loved her college life. Carol's health remained about the same, with periodic crashes and naps required every day. Major tensions developed with neighbors on all sides, and two years later we moved to a house on ten acres, with no neighbors in sight in any direction. Luckily we were able to sell the Brighton house soon after buying the new home.

We loved the new home on Pounds Court. At this time, we had four dogs, so we named the place "The Dog Pound," and posted a sign with that moniker at the end of our long private driveway. The home had an oversized three-car garage, and Carol decided that we would convert one of the garages into a heated space for her car, which could also be used as a bedroom/game room when Ellen was home from college. The house had a nice in-ground pool, which ironically was the fourth home that we had owned with a pool. I was getting pretty darn good at pool maintenance. The place had a huge eight-horse stall barn, with a big middle section that easily held our boat, as well as many of the beat-up cars and trucks that Patrick would buy and tinker with over the coming years. Patrick and I both got dirt bikes, and we spent time riding together in the woods behind our house, and on trails up north. We started an annual tradition of going skiing in Colorado, just us boys, over President's Day weekend. Patrick excelled in auto shop at school, and was always working on one of his cars or trucks in our garage.

In late 2006 Ralph Jackson, my father-in-law, died after a long, courageous struggle with cancer. I spoke at his funeral, sharing how Ralph had influenced my life and was such a huge mentor. He was a true hero to me, not only because of his time as a fighter pilot and POW in World War II, but also in the way he lived his life after returning home from the service. After Ralph died, I felt a clear sense of, "Brett, it's now time to step up and be an adult." I no longer had someone to turn to for advice, and had to make my own decisions from now on.

Later that year, Dana turned 21. Carol and I decided to take her and a friend on a trip to celebrate her birthday. We were all excited to go have some fun in Las Vegas!

It's now 5 a.m. Still pitch dark in this room.

Drip—drip—drip.

I hear sirens in the distance, and a faint sliver of light peeks in through the curtains. I look out and down to the street. There are several women in short skirts, smoking and talking with each other, loitering around the street light. I wonder about their lives—selling their bodies for a living. Are their parents alive? Do they have children? What happened to them? Then I wonder about my life. That dread comes back and covers me like a heavy blanket. After I read through all the work emails, I click on *Tom Hill's Friday Eaglezine* and start to read it. I know this is a waste of time, but I'm not feeling very productive, and at five in the morning, what does it matter anyway?

My life is about to change.

Chapter Two: Awakening

Born in rural Missouri in 1935, his beginnings were far from remarkable. The son of a turkey farmer, little Tom Hill was exposed to a loving family and hard work, but not much else outside of Adair County, Missouri. That was true until his father bought a Cessna 170 four-seat tail dragger airplane which would be used to deliver turkeys. Fifteen-year-old Tom and his brother Roger, out of economic necessity, learned to fly that Cessna and used it to deliver their father's turkeys all across the Midwest.

Taking off and landing from the field behind their farm house was an adventure, especially when landing at night. To accomplish this daring feat, Tom and Roger would fly the plane low, barely over the farmhouse, to wake up his parents and to scare off any cattle that may be loitering on the grass runway. Tom's dad would then drive the old pickup around to the field, aim the headlights down the grass strip, and provide some illumination for the boys to land the plane. It was during these years that Tom started to see the difference between turkeys (the dumbest animals on earth—according to Dr. Hill), and the incredible power and potential of flight.

After graduating from a high school class of 127, Tom went on to college at the University of Missouri. After his sophomore year, Tom dropped out of school for a year to teach junior high and high school. Realizing this was not for him, Tom went back and finished his degree at Mizzou. While at college, at nineteen years old, he met a cute girl named Carol, and was soon married. Tom went on to get his master's degree, and along with the education and work experience came four healthy children. Next was a PhD in education from the University of Missouri, and a promotion to the position of regional director of the University of Missouri Extension Service. For Tom, life was progressing well and the future looked promising. Or did it? Something was wrong. Tom felt a tugging in his soul that there must be something more. He loved his wife and children—that was an absolute. What he didn't love was the career path in which he found himself. He knew there was more, but couldn't articulate it. He felt an urge to grow, to stretch his wings, to be more like a Cessna, and less like a turkey. Tom started to become interested in personal development and reading. He reached out to some folks whom he respected at work, who gave him some suggestions on how to achieve more. He was getting restless. About this time, Tom and Carol started to experience stress in their marriage. Tom's itch to grow and to do more in his life was different than Carol's goals. A wonderful mother and wife, Carol was completely happy in the stable life that the two had built. After a couple of years of struggle, marriage counseling, and prayer, Tom and Carol divorced in 1976.

Divorce was not part of Tom's life plan. Growing up a strong Southern Baptist, divorce was just not an acceptable course of action. Everyone thought Tom was crazy. They thought he was being selfish. It took years for Tom to recover—to rebuild and gain his sense of direction and purpose. During this time his career as an academic thrived and he was promoted regularly within the university system. Feeling the guilt of putting his four children in a split-family, Tom tried hard to maintain a close relationship with all four kids, and do what he could to be a good dad as they all grew up too fast.

* * *

It's now 7 a.m., and the sun is starting to rise. For the past thirty minutes, I've watched as the colors of the dawning sky erase the panorama of the neon jungle below my hotel room window. The buzz in this city is crazy, and I'm amazed at how people can actually live here. I can barely survive just a few days. My mind has been churning with thoughts of what I'm going to do now. After reading the *Eaglezine*, something happened inside me, and I now feel a new and overwhelming sense of calm and confidence. It's as if something heavy and dark has been lifted from me. I know, at this moment, that I am going to quit my job at AFL. I feel serene in my knowing that this is the right move for me. I'm alert, I'm focused, and I'm completely at peace. I'm also completely without a plan of what to do next. Having worked now for almost twenty years for the same company, I don't know how people go about finding new jobs these days. I think I want to get out of automotive, but something in manufacturing is probably right for me. I'm thinking that my combination of an engineering degree and an MBA, plus hopefully my work experience, will be the right stuff for some other company. The thought of sitting down and writing my resume sounds daunting. Carol will still be asleep for a couple of hours, and I'm dreading telling her about what just happened. Maybe I won't. I'm not sure how she'll react when I tell her that I'm going to quit my job, but I'm pretty sure that she'll want to move out of Michigan. My guess is she'll want to head back to Nashville. She loves it there.

* * *

When Carol did wake up, I decided to go ahead and tell her. I was simply too excited to hold it back. After sharing with her what had happened when I woke up earlier that morning, I was surprised at how well she took it. She was unusually calm, and said, "I trust you. I have full confidence in you. Whatever you choose to do, I'm sure you'll do great." Wow. That was not what I expected, and I felt even better about the decision I had made. I also knew that I had an obligation to make it work, for Carol and for the family. Now, what to do next?

After returning back to Brighton and back to the office, the dread of my job hit me smack in the face. I was surprised, caught completely off guard, by the news of a big reorganization, which included me being shifted to work under one of my previous co-workers. Mike was a great guy, super-smart and excellent at his job, but he was a few years younger than me. We had been peers for several years, and I simply couldn't stomach the thought of being his subordinate. It felt as if this was somehow reassurance of the decision that I had made that early morning in Las Vegas. My entire sense of self-worth was deflated with the thought that my career growth at AFL had now plateaued. Could this be the beginning of the end of my professional growth? This was something that I absolutely could not accept. These feelings were new to me, but they were intense and they were real. Now it was clearly time to get busy.

Upon reading the *Eaglezine* that early November morning in Las Vegas, I was brought back to the time twenty years prior when Tom Hill and I, along with Vicki Mizerez, joined forces to sell RE/MAX real estate franchises in South Georgia. In this particular issue of the *Eaglezine*, Tom tells the story of how he quit his job at the University of Missouri, a job that he could not get fired from, and joined his college buddy in the RE/MAX adventure. In the first two weeks of rejection-filled cold call sales of this unique business concept, Tom had not made a single sale. He had difficulty getting people even willing to make an appointment to listen to his pitch. He was starting to wonder if this thing would work for him.

On the Friday of his second week of prospecting, Tom got up, showered, dressed in coat and tie, and stepped out of his little camper trailer to march to his truck. Slipping on the rainy step, Tom fell flat on his face, landing in mud and leaves, with cold rain pelting on the back of his neck. Murmuring to himself, he said, "Tom Hill, are you crazy? You left a job at the university that you could not get fired from, and for what? For this?" Tom could have easily gone back into his trailer, cleaned up, given up, and driven straight back to Missouri. Instead, he got mad, he returned into his little camper-trailer, cleaned up, went back out on his prospecting route, and ended up making the first RE/MAX sale of his career that afternoon. Had Tom given up that rainy morning, he would have missed out on an amazing journey that would change Tom's and Betty's lives beyond their wildest imaginations. That day in Augusta, Georgia, and that event with Tom's face in the mud, was the turning point for his new career and new life.

In reading that story, sitting at my laptop in a Las Vegas hotel room, I immediately felt a connection that sparked me into action. In Tom's story, he was 50 years old when he made his big life change. I was reading this at 45 years old, but I somehow felt much older than that. I could absolutely relate to Tom's story. Was I going through a mid-life crisis? I didn't know what it was, but I felt free. I felt alive. I felt vibrant and excited. Excited for the first time in many, many years.

I was still lost on what to do next. I wrote my resume, which was as difficult as I had thought it would be. I emailed it to a few recruiters that I knew. I was right about Carol. She wanted to move back to Nashville, or if not Nashville, somewhere warm. This meant that a job in Michigan was out of the question, which was unfortunate given most of my experience was in the automotive industry and most of my professional contacts lived in the area. After a few weeks of not getting any realistic job leads from the few recruiters I knew, I decided I had better start networking.

I began actually reading the Friday *Eaglezines*, and lo-and-behold, the one that next Friday morning featured Tom's unique networking system. It dawned on me that I should reach out to Tom and see if he had any advice on my job search. I wrote him a short email explaining what I was thinking, hoping he would get back to me soon. By this time I had told my boss at work I wanted to leave, and that I felt that the company could use the cost reduction of my salary in other more valuable ways. Mike took the news amazingly well, and I think that as a friend he understood the situation that I was in. What a relief. Mike agreed to let me stay on as long as I wanted while I figured out what my next move would be.

Tom Hill emailed me back within a couple of hours. I was thrilled that he was so open to helping me, and his email had one assignment. He asked me to email him back, telling him what's been going on in my life, and to "let it flow," sharing whatever was on my mind. This seemed strange to me, but I'm a rule follower, so I did what he said. Tom also asked me to tell him what kind of companies and what kind of roles I wanted to do, and also what I did not want to do. This also was surprisingly difficult, but I took the time to do what he asked. My response to Tom was that I wanted to work for a large manufacturing company, and that the roles I would be interested in included:

- Human Resources
- Logistics
- Purchasing
- Project Management
- Quality
- Trade Compliance

The roles that I definitely wanted nothing to do with were:

- Sales
- Marketing
- Finance

I obviously didn't know myself well. The roles that I thought that I didn't want to do, especially sales and marketing, eventually became enjoyable roles best suited for my personal strengths and interests.

A few days later Tom and I scheduled a phone call, and we had a wonderful time catching up. Tom and Betty were now living in St. Louis, and Tom was spending most of his time coaching entrepreneurs and giving presentations to Vistage and other groups around the country. He also had recently co-authored *Chicken Soup for the Entrepreneur's Soul*. Tom was excited about an online coaching program that he had developed and recently released. After going through the list of occupations I could see myself doing, and the other jobs that I wanted to stay far, far away from, Tom dropped another bomb into my life. He asked, "Have you considered working for yourself?"

This question caught me off-guard, and I had to pause a while before I answered. "Well, not since I was a kid, unless you count the time we worked together during the RE/MAX days." Tom and I reminisced about that year of working together, and we recalled the day when we ran 10 miles around Tybee Island. That run just about killed me, and I was humbled that a 50-year-old man, double my age, could actually outrun me. Tom said to me, "Brett, if running your own business is an option, then now is a good time to consider it."

Tom's question cracked open a vault that had been shut for over two decades. As a young child, I used to dream about one day running my own business. I remember wanting to invent something. Something really big that would somehow change the world. I wanted to write a novel. I loved working with people, and meeting new people. Then I made a big mistake. A huge mistake. I decided to get an engineering degree and pursue a technical path in the corporate world. My time at 3M was short, and dissatisfaction led me to take Tom Hill's opportunity to follow him to Georgia on the RE/MAX path. I was a terrible RE/MAX franchise salesperson.

I tried hard, I learned a lot, and I grew during that year. But I was simply unable to close the deals. I now know that my lack of self-esteem, along with my negative programming about salespeople in general, poured into me when I was a very small child, were huge barriers to my success in sales. My upbringing as well as my failure as a salesperson during the RE/MAX years were both part of why I said, "No way," to a sales-related role. The thought of owning my own business, however, was starting to reignite a flame that yearned to be lit.

I followed Tom's advice about networking, and started reaching out to friends and colleagues about what I should do next. I was keeping the option open of doing something entrepreneurial. In phone calls to two different friends, Marsha and Mike, within the same afternoon, I was blown away by their advice. Both friends told me that they thought I should be a recruiter. A recruiter? You've got to be kidding me! Why in the world would I do that? I know nothing about recruiting, and I can't imagine spending all day "selling" to people. I told both of my friends that I thought they were completely out of their minds. That evening my head started spinning. Why in the world would two different people, on the same afternoon, suggest the same crazy idea? When I asked Marsha why she suggested being a recruiter, she said that I was great with people, that my human resources experience would be a huge plus, and that she knew I would work hard and be successful. Marsha was our real estate agent back in Tennessee, so through the many homes that we bought and sold with Marsha's help, she knew me fairly well. I didn't realize when I called her that she was now a recruiter, so she had some experience from which to make the recommendation. Mike had pretty much the same advice, although his frame of reference came from the different recruiters he worked with in his corporate roles. I didn't know it at the time, but I had just experienced what would be a recurring theme of enjoying "predictable miracles," or synchronicity as I would later be taught by Dr. Hill.

Recruiting? Now that was about as far away from something that I would consider as anything. By this time I was looking at maybe buying a franchise like Subway or a bagel shop, but found out that these types of businesses need huge amounts of money to get started, and they take forever to make any real money. I didn't have all that much money to invest and I knew I needed to make a decent living, and fast. Recruiting? How do I either rule this in or rule this out? Oh yeah—Michael Soulek back in San Antonio had a recruiting company, or at least that's what I think he did.

Carol and I became friends with Michael and his wife,

Susan, who both went to our church. We had been invited to their big, beautiful home on a cliff in the Hill Country, and also to a couple of San Antonio Spurs games. I knew he was a great guy, a strong Christian, had a wonderful family, and had some kind of business called FoodPro. I also knew he drove a very nice car. It had been several years since Michael and I had talked, and I mustered up the courage to call him. He answered the phone, we had a great time catching up, and it felt as if no time at all had passed. I asked Michael if his business was in recruiting, and he said yes, and that he specializes in the food industry. He shared with me how he got into the field, and how he now goes about his work. Planning and personal discipline were the two key things that he emphasized. Michael was reassuring, and he said that he thought I'd be good at this profession. I then talked with my friend Marsha, who had now been a recruiter for several years, and she gave me the same type of feedback and encouragement. It started to seem like going into recruiting was the right path. But how?

By this time I had shared my thoughts with another friend in Detroit who owned a recruiting company. He was generous in showing me around his office, and ultimately he offered to hire and train me. After considering this for a few days, it hit me that the major reason I wanted to own a business in the first place was to be my own boss. The idea of working for someone else again was simply not part of the equation. So if I am not going to work for someone else, how do I get started? I bought a couple of books on recruiting and running a recruiting firm, and soon became overwhelmed with all of the details and intricacies of getting started.

At AFL, things were now lining up to where I would be laid off from the company, and as part of this, I would receive severance for the twenty years that I had worked there. That would be a huge help in my transition, but the transition to what? I finally realized that I didn't know enough about the recruiting business to hang my own shingle, and that I probably should go the franchise route. At this time there were six recruiting franchise firms that seemed like they might work, and I made visits to four of them to check things out. The last franchise that I visited was Akron, Ohio-based Sanford Rose Associates (SRA). Upon meeting the owner and getting a first-hand look at the business and its philosophies, I immediately knew this was the right choice for me. What attracted me most to SRA was that the business was modeled around mid-career professionals, like myself, who moved from industry into executive search, leveraging their prior education, experience, and network into a relationship-based search firm, as opposed to a high-volume transactional business. I knew that I liked people, I liked developing lasting relationships, and this model seemed very attractive.

I bought my franchise in April 2007, and opened Sanford Rose Associates–Howell (Michigan) on June 1, 2007. In my last few weeks at AFL, knowing that I had purchased my recruiting franchise and what my direction was going to be, I could hardly contain my enthusiasm. Apparently my excitement was contagious, as my co-worker Kirk Nelson, who was also increasingly unhappy with things at AFL, chose to resign from his job and join me as a non-equity business partner in my new venture. Kirk and I settled into our little one-room office in the Howell Chamber of Commerce building, and thus began my new life as an entrepreneur.

Before opening the doors to the business on June 1, 2007, I attended two weeks of on-site training at the SRA headquarters in Akron, Ohio. This was amazing training, and I left with everything I needed to get started. I also had a couple of weeks to get the office organized, and to ponder on other things. Reaching back out to Tom Hill to let him know how things had progressed, Tom asked if I had any interest in signing up for his online coaching program. At only $35 per month, and given I had a pretty large amount of money sitting in my checking account after getting my severance check, I said sure, not at all knowing what this would mean. I would one day recognize that this decision meant more than I could dream. Tom also sent a copy of his book, *Living at the Summit* as well as *Chicken Soup for the Entrepreneur's Soul*. I crawled through both books, as I was a very, very slow reader. As I read *Living at the Summit*, I questioned what prompted Tom to write such a book. I knew that he was successful in his transition from egghead professor (his words) to successful entrepreneur, but I had no idea that he had such a whole-life approach to what it means to achieve success. The book, told in a story format, revealed to me Tom's real motivations.

By being part of his online program, called E-goal Bronze, I looked forward to receiving my coaching lesson every Monday morning. Early in the process was an assignment to determine my life's priorities, and to assess my balance in each of the areas. My life was clearly way out of balance, and I saw this for the very first time. Another assignment for the week was to write down my "perfect day" six years in the future, writing in intricate detail, with all the senses (sight, smell, touch, taste, sound) involved. Whew—this was difficult, but being the dutiful follower I am trained to be, I did what was assigned. Not too much later, the lessons started to delve into goal setting and a concept called the G-Curve (more on the G-Curve in Chapter Ten).

In my first few weeks of work with SRA, I started emailing and calling everyone I knew, sharing the exciting news of my new venture. A lot of people whom I had previously worked with thought that I was completely crazy. Others were jealous. Most were indifferent.

> I was actually empowered to design a life, to design MY LIFE!

I was overly concerned in what each was feeling, and this got in my way. I kept on going, and soon found success in winning some big recruiting projects with some previous co-workers. Even though I was doing well financially, something seemed wrong. I had so quickly moved from the corporate world, saddled with all the structure, meetings, protocols, and more meetings … to a world with none of this. While the freedom to set my own schedule and chart my own path at my new career was exhilarating, it was also uncomfortable. I found that the lack of structure to my day, and actually to my life, was making me feel slippery, rudderless, a little out of control.

The weekly coaching lessons from the E-goal Bronze program was a great source of structure. I began to notice, for the very first time in my life, that I was actually empowered to design a life, to design MY LIFE! I began to walk taller, to raise my head, and actually look into the future—way, way into the future. This was new for me, a direction that I had not looked into since way back, perhaps as far back as elementary school. I was scared. I was excited. I was growing and stretching and blessed to have some help.

Chapter Three: Hubris of Success

Money is falling out of the sky.

Is this how life goes for the successful entrepreneur? This is amazing! Why did I wait so long to do this? I'm going to be rich, and it's so dang easy.

* * *

That's what I thought, and that's how things went the first six months of running my new recruiting business. Not having any sales training or experience, other than that tough year with RE/MAX, I set out to tell everyone I knew about the new business I was in. My business was simple; companies would pay me money if they hired someone I found and "presented" to them for specific roles. My fee was somewhere between 20 and 25 percent of the new employee's annual salary. This could be a pretty big figure, as many of the positions I recruited for had salaries of over $100,000.

My first recruiting project was with a company based in Washington, D.C. The company was being run by a guy I knew from my previous days with AFL. As part of my "call everybody I knew" approach to marketing, I picked up the phone and called Mark. He was happy to take my call, and after catching up on our personal lives, the conversation soon shifted to business. Mark liked to talk, so I listened as he went on and on about things with his firm. I later figured out that my secret to sales is to be a great listener. Mark finally asked me what I was doing work-wise, and I let him know. He said, "Man, you sure called at the right time! We need to hire a controller." The company that Mark was now working for was a pioneer in creating and selling classes and training for "information technology security professionals." I had no idea what an IT security training company did, nor did I have any experience with financial positions like a controller. Before I could comment, Mark said, "I suspect you work on a retainer, so is a fee of around thirty percent okay with you?" I couldn't believe what I was hearing. My heart started to race. After taking a couple of deep breaths, I calmly said, "Yes, I can work with that. How about one-third of the fee up front, another third after we've presented a slate of candidates and the final payment when the candidate starts work?"

Mark's reply was, "Sounds good." When I hung up the phone, I high-fived my business partner Kirk, and then quickly realized I had a problem.

I had no idea how to find candidates for a controller position with an IT security training company based in Washington, D.C. I'm an ex-engineer with a human resources background. I've worked most of my career at an automotive parts supplier based in Detroit. I did what I was recently trained to do— call SRA corporate for help. Lo-and-behold, I was advised to "split" this recruiting project with another SRA office, one which specialized in recruiting for finance-related positions. Six weeks later, after interviewing four candidates, the IT security training company hired one of our candidates, and the other SRA office owner and I split a total fee of $33,000. Wow, $16,500 for making a phone call and coordinating some interviews—now that was some serious money.

This transaction was indicative of how the overall business went that glorious first year. Several high-dollar recruiting projects easily came my way, most of which we were able to complete with our internal team, and avoid the cost of splitting with outside offices. To keep up with the growing business, I quickly hired additional people, including a full-time administrative assistant and several part-time recruiters. The days were full of activity in our tiny little office, and the future looked promising.

I was enjoying going through the weekly online coaching program that I had purchased. Every couple of months I would have a quick phone call with Tom Hill to let him know how things were going, and he sounded about as excited as I was with how well my new business was developing. We had fun reflecting on some of the early days we shared in trying to sell RE/MAX real estate franchises back in Georgia and Kentucky some 22 years prior.

In one of our talks, Tom asked if I thought I'd enjoy having a coach help me along with my weekly lessons. Tom had several experts on his team providing in-person coaching for a number of his clients, and he sensed that I may be at a point that this would accelerate my growth. The cost of $95 per month seemed reasonable to me, so I said, "Sure, let's do it." Jim Nissen became my coach, and over the next six months, he helped me in a number of ways, but most importantly, Jim helped me recognize some of my emotional barriers to the sales process. As a retired, very successful insurance salesman, Jim had the real-life experience and his own path of growth that I could relate to. During this period of working regularly with Jim as my life coach, my business continued to grow, and I started to grow as a person as well.

Tom called one day out of the blue. He has a way of doing this. I've learned not to be so surprised any more. Tom said, "Brett, would you like to join me and be a Hell's Angel?" What? I thought he must be joking, but somehow his voice didn't sound like he was. I knew Tom had ridden a Harley Davidson in his younger years, but a Hell's Angel? You gotta be kidding me!

I said, "Tom, I don't even own a street bike." Tom knew that Patrick and I both had off-road motorcycles and we liked to go dirt-biking on the weekends.

Tom chuckled. "I didn't say 'Hell's Angel.' I said 'Hill's Angel.'"

I asked, "What is a Hill's Angel?" Tom went on to explain that he had been personally coaching thirty high-performing entrepreneurs, and that one of his coaching clients had decided to retire and leave the program, creating space for a new member to the group. Tom shared that he was impressed with my fast success as a new entrepreneur, that he had full confidence in my ongoing and future success, and that I "had what it takes" to be a Hill's Angel. I was shocked. I had not remotely considered being honored in such a way. The cost: $450 per month, with no contract and I could stop any time. Four hundred fifty dollars per month? Now that's talking some real change. That's a very nice car payment. That's a couple of vacations each year. But, maybe, just maybe, this will help me grow even faster than I would otherwise, and help my business be more successful. I said, "Sure, let's do it" to being a "Hill's Angel," and decided I'd monitor how things went over time. I'd do the math in a few months to see if I earned more incremental money than the cost of the coaching fee. Little did I know at the time that making more money, which I

> " My life was starting to change in nearly every aspect. "

certainly did, was the least impacted area in my life as a result of becoming a Hill's Angel.

My life was starting to change in nearly every aspect. I noticed that I would wake up earlier in the mornings and with excitement and anticipation of what each new day would bring. I was energized as I began, for the very first time in my life, to actually take charge in planning, designing and living my personal, authentic, and hopefully long and exceptional life.

The monthly coaching calls with Tom quickly started to make a difference. I was changing. In the very first call, Tom gave me the assignment to describe in writing, in minute detail, a perfect day in my perfect life six years into the future. I had already completed a similar exercise as part of the 52 weekly lessons, but I didn't put too much effort into that assignment the first time. There was no one to read it, no one to turn it in to, so I glossed by it fairly quickly. This time, with Tom being the recipient, and me not wanting to let him down, now that I was a "Hill's Angel" and all, I put a ton of thought and effort into the assignment. After getting it written, and then in reviewing it with Tom, the result became obvious. The gap between what my life was at that time, and what my perfect life looked like six years into the future, represented the things that needed my intention and focus.

I'm an engineer, at least by formal education. I struggled through many of the engineering classes in college, and hated my engineering jobs. I got my MBA and moved as quickly as possible and as far away as I could get from technical roles. However, through my training and early experience, I learned to be very organized and disciplined, both traits that would serve me well in the coming years. I took on this new coaching process with a passion, and applied to it the structure of a dedicated engineer. I created Microsoft Excel sheets to organize my goals, and made circle and line graphs to illustrate and track my progress. As part of my coaching relationship, I shared these documents with liberal arts professor Tom, whom I think found this engineer-headed structure to be, in one his favorite terms, "fascinating."

From the very beginning, Tom taught me to observe and evaluate my life according to the areas that were most important. Setting these areas of life, these priorities, was another difficult challenge, similar to visioning and writing down my future perfect life. Tom shared with me the six priorities that he and his wife, Betty had jointly agreed upon many, many years before when he was with the university. I couldn't come up with a better list, and in respect to the amazing lives that Tom and Betty had created I decided to go along with their list. Their areas of life, in priority order, were:

- Spiritual
- Physical Health
- Relationships
- Emotional
- Intellectual/Professional
- Financial

Tom asked me to draw a circle with six spokes, each spoke representing one of the priority areas of my life. Then I had to rate my current life, on a scale of zero to 10, with 10 being perfect, on each of the criteria. This was difficult and extremely painful. I had never thought about my life in these ways. Doing so felt completely selfish. It felt like a total waste of time. I had way too many other things to be doing. Or did I? Another part of my brain, or maybe my soul, was whispering to me. Was my hesitancy born of fear? Was I afraid to grow, to be authentic? Was I afraid to be honest and proceed with my correct path? What if my current path was the wrong path? What if I've lied to myself all these years? What if I've been living someone else's life? My head was being jumbled, and I refocused on the assignment.

My Circle of Life looked like this:

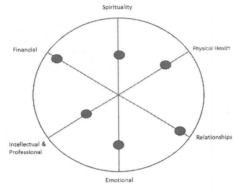

Given how well my new business had done since I left that dreaded job at AFL only six-months prior, I believed that things in my life were going pretty well. From all outside measures, things looked great. I had just received a boatload of money in severance, cashed in stock options at a record price, paid cash for a brand new Ford F-150 Crew Cab pickup, and was making more money than ever in my "making money from thin air" executive recruiting business. On the wheel of life, I immediately went to the "Financial" line, and humbly gave myself a rating of nine as my score. Wait—according to Tom's philosophies, the financial rating should come last, and be the lowest priority. I've heard Tom say that if someone is functioning very well and is balanced on the five other areas of life (Spiritual, Physical Health, Relationships, Emotional, and Intellectual/Professional) then the "Financial" part will somehow just take care of itself. Tom says that you don't pursue money, that money pursues you, based upon how valuable you become in the marketplace.

So why did I naturally start this evaluation process with immediate reflection on how well I was doing financially? Was it because that was where I was putting most of my attention? Maybe because my ego was pumped up by how well things were going financially at that time? Maybe because some of the other areas in my life weren't going all that well, and I didn't want to face them? I got a brief glimpse of recognition there were indeed other areas of my life that I didn't want to dig into, areas that had been buried over the years with pain and neglect.

Tom's "Circle of Life" process then requires a game of "connect-the-dots." By connecting the dots in my circle, I would be able to see my overall degree of balance and have a tool from which to identify the areas that would need my most immediate attention.

My picture now looked like this:

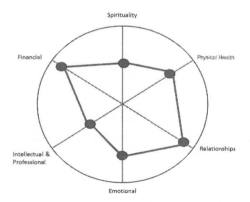

A balanced life, when the dots are connected, should look like a circle—like a wheel. A wheel rolls smoothly down the road only because it is a perfect circle. Any other shape brings with it repeated bumpiness. Wow! I did not like the shape of my wheel.

I began, for the very first time, to take a hard, honest look at how I was living my life. I knew I had a good life, a successful life, but was it my authentic life? Why was I doing the things I was doing? I knew that choosing to be an industrial engineer right out of high school was a mistake. What other mistakes have I made? What mistakes am I making right now? I wondered how much of my current life was the result of conscious choices I had actually made? Was I addressing my passions, or was I simply living a life according to other people's expectations? I didn't like the thoughts crossing my mind, nor the realization that was taking place.

> Most of my adult life had been lived as if my life course was on autopilot—to a destination programmed by other people's expectations.

It became clear to me that most of my adult life had been lived as if my life course was on autopilot—set on a destination programmed by other people's expectations. Had I been blind to my own real purpose these past twenty years? Had I been lying to myself as I acted "happy" in my life and my career all this time? Are these new supposed "priorities" really all that important and in this specific order?

1 – Spirituality
2 – Physical Health
3 – Relationships
4 – Emotions
5 – Intellectual and Professional
6 – Financial

I decided to go ahead and say, "Yes," these are to be the primary areas in my life, and that I would initially prioritize them in this order. By making this decision it was clear that I had a ton of work to do, and that true life balance seemed a long way away.

Reverting back to my organized engineer-self, I created an Excel sheet, and made headings for each of the six areas of life, along with my current score for each. I then typed in the things that I would do in each of the areas to improve my score—to improve in that specific area of my life.

I started with the "Spiritual" category, as that was now supposed to be number one in my life, and ironically, it was also my lowest rating on the circle. As a family we were members of Hartland All-Saints Lutheran Church. We went at least once per month, sometimes twice. I'd throw a twenty into the offering plate, feeling somewhat generous. We always went on Easter and Christmas. We loved the candlelight service on Christmas Eve. I tried to remember to every morning say the *Prayer of Jabez* combined with my rote-memorized Eagle Scout prayer. Anything else? Not really.

Tom Hill defines spirituality as a personal realization, a knowing, that there is something bigger than ourselves in the universe. That there is a higher power. Tom makes a distinction between "spirituality" and "religion." Spirituality relates to an individual's connection to and relationship with a greater power. Religion relates to an organized approach to spirituality. Tom believes that we are all spiritual beings having a very brief physical experience here on earth. Some people believe that they are simply physical beings sometimes having spiritual experiences. There are profound differences between

> We are all spiritual beings having a very brief physical experience here on earth.

the two different ways of thinking. **❝ I decided to make a habit of changing my habits. ❞** Where do I sit?

As I pondered this question, I started to look deep within. I recognized that not only did I believe, but I knew that I was and am a spiritual being having a short physical experience. Hopefully not too short. There is a part of me that has a strong connection to birds in flight, and I've had powerful dreams where I am flying or floating above the earth. I love flight—birds, airplanes, hot air balloons, kites—and I wonder if I was somehow a bird in a previous life.

So—how do I grow in my spirituality? I decided to create new habits. Tom had shown me that so much in life is about our habits. Most of our habits are on autopilot from how we were raised as small children. Other habits develop along the way, usually unconsciously. The best habits are made from choices and discipline. I decided to make a habit of changing my habits.

My new spiritual habits were going to be:

- Heartfelt prayer every day
- Read from the Bible every day
- Read other books on spirituality
- Get more involved at church

Praying every day was already almost a habit, but my prayers were a memorized recital. I realized this wasn't doing the trick, so I worked to have my new prayers be a conversation with God, and share what was really on my mind and in my heart. I found that this was a fantastic way to grow in my authentic relationship with Him.

Reading from the Bible was difficult, but after buying *The*

Message translation, I found that the contemporary language used in this version made so much more sense to me. I have been a Christian my entire life, but reading the Bible in this way brought into understanding Jesus's words and teachings in a way I had never previously considered.

I began to buy books, especially books on spiritual growth. I have become a huge fan of Dr. Wayne Dyer, and have read every book he's written. Other great spiritual authors I've appreciated are Deepak Chopra, Eckhart Tolle, Paulo Coelho, and Miguel Ruiz.

I offered to volunteer as a co-leader of the high school youth group at church. Not long after starting in this role, the primary youth group leader decided he needed to take some time off to deal with business challenges, so I became the sole leader. I loved this role, and grew immensely in my spirituality, and in my skills as a leader. I also recognized my innate love for teaching and for helping younger folks. This caused me to tap into one of my true passions—helping people.

The next lowest rating in my Circle of Life was in the area of "Intellectual/Professional." The definition for this rating was "continuous learning, professional growth and mastery." Even though I was making a lot of money in my new career, I wasn't honestly learning much. Outside of the quick rush to learn how to start a recruiting business, there hadn't been much new that I've learned since I got my MBA during night school in 1990. I remembered how much I enjoyed going back to college, and was able to juggle work, being a husband, and a father to two little girls plus a baby boy on the way. Patrick was born just weeks before my final class at Tennessee State University and graduating with my MBA. The timing on that big life change was perfect.

I had also since receiving my MBA learned Spanish and

German. I did this by having a Berlitz tutor come to my office, usually once a week. I had previously learned Japanese while living in Tokyo during college and for the two years back at Mizzou after I returned. I recalled how much I enjoyed studying and learning new languages, and the thrill I'd get in trying to use the languages at restaurants, on vacation, and sometimes during business trips.

> Why did I quit learning new things?

What happened since then? Why did I quit learning new things? I love learning, but somehow forgot that. I realized that all I was doing these days was "doing." I decided that I needed to set some goals and develop some new habits around learning.

"I read a book a day, sometimes two." He said that without flinching. How in the world could Tom Hill actually read one full book every day? I asked him about that, and he shared his secret with me. "Learn to read faster and read only good books—books that you'll be interested in and will help you grow," he said. "Replace the television with reading, and make it all a habit." I was a very slow reader, crawling through pages at 250 words per minute. At this pace, there was no way in hell that I could read a book a month, let alone a book a day.

Tom suggested I try an inexpensive computerized program called EyeQ, which I did, and I quickly improved my reading speed to over 500 words per minute, doubling my original speed. Continuing with EyeQ for another year, I improved my reading speed to over 1200 words per minute. It was amazing that as my reading speed improved, without any loss of comprehension, not only did I read many more books, but I also fell in love with reading. I signed up for Amazon and then Amazon Prime, and with the app on my iPhone, I can one-click purchase any book that is either recommended or that I somehow come upon that fits one of my areas of interest. My Amazon book buying habit is my crack, but it's an addiction that I'm willing to maintain in pursuit of an exceptional life.

With respect to growing in the "Professional" side of the "Intellectual/Professional" part of the Circle of Life, I decided that I would become the very best recruiter that I could be. How? By getting just a little bit better each and every day. Jim Rohn is quoted as saying that if in one year a person reads one hour per day on any particular subject they will be in the top 10 percent of people in the world in that subject. I took that suggestion literally by buying books on the recruiting profession, and committing myself to daily reading and growth in this new field. I knew I wasn't the smartest recruiter in the market, and I certainly didn't have natural sales skills, but I figured I could outwork anyone. I quickly became one of the top performers in the SRA network, and was soon asked to serve as an adjunct instructor teaching new SRA office owners how to best start their new businesses. I was also asked to contribute articles for the *Fordyce Letter*, a monthly newsletter popular within the recruiting profession.

Recognizing the growth that was taking place in my life, Tom Hill asked if I would be a presenter at his Eagle Summit gathering soon to take place in Milwaukee, Wisconsin. I nervously accepted that challenge, and gave a one-hour presentation to a group of about one hundred high performing entrepreneurs. Reading from my notes and using PowerPoint slides as a crutch, I survived that presentation. I was overwhelmed by the amount of genuine applause and appreciation I received for my story. Those other Hill's Angels sure are nice folks, I rationalized. A year later, with more growth under my belt, I gave a follow-up presentation to another gathering of Eagles at the Eagle Summit in New Brunswick, Canada. Again, I was amazed by the great reception I received.

Having set some goals on the "Spiritual" and "Intellectual/ Professional" parts of my lopsided Circle of Life, I still needed to pay attention to the other areas. The "Emotional" and "Physical Health" areas of my life were the next areas of deficit. Following Tom's insistence that I set measurable goals in each of the six areas of life, I pondered what goals to set for the "Physical Health" measure. I was surprised that Tom put this area as the number two most important area in his life—ahead of even his relationship with Betty and his kids. I asked Tom about this, and he said that yes, he and Betty totally agreed that their physical health was more important than anything, other than their relationships with God. "Without vibrant physical health, without energy and stamina and independence—how can I be the very best I can be?" Tom said. "If I am sick or weak and can't take care of myself, then I will become a burden to my family or to society in general."

According to Tom, a strong, healthy, vibrant body (and mind) is absolutely critical in living an exceptional life. Tom speaks often about OIYF, short

> OIYF—Put the Odds In Your Favor.

for "Putting the Odds in Your Favor." I've learned to respect these four letters. On the "Physical Health" side of life, OIYF refers to doing the basic things, on a daily basis, to improve the odds that you will have a long, healthy life. Examples are simple, and somewhat boring to most people, but profound in their impact over time. Eat healthy foods. Get regular exercise. Get plenty of sleep. Have annual physical exams and deal proactively with health challenges. Our culture does not make these things easy. The grocery stores and fast-food chains are stocked full of foods that will promote chronic illness over time. Our television and internet-addicted culture primed with its immediate-results mentality make the commitment to long-term daily exercise incredibly difficult.

I began to realize that I was living a life that was mediocre on the health front. While not overweight and moderately athletic, I was choosing unhealthy foods and certainly not getting regular exercise. Tom suggested that I set health-related goals for the next 18 months. I soon learned much more about this special number—18.

He pushed me to come up with one big health related goal that would stretch me outside my comfort zone. Thinking about this, I remembered how much I hated running cross-country in high school. I did this only to get in shape before wrestling season started, and because Coach Sears demanded that his varsity wrestlers either play football or run cross-county prior to the wresting season. I was way too small for football, so a distance runner I became. Did I mention I hated running? We had to wear skimpy little shorts and flat running shoes, and our training and competitions were often times in sub-freezing cold or rainy weather. Coach Parker would send the team out on long street runs to warm up, and he would drive around in his Corvette, yelling out his window at us to speed up. I'll never forget him sneaking up behind me one day on the street, while I was running down a big, long hill. In his whiny voice, Coach Parker barked out, "Stride out, Blair—stride out!"

Several years later, while working for Tom Hill on the RE/MAX journey, he invited me to run with him on the beach one beautiful morning at Tybee Island, Georgia. Tom was 50, I was 25. As we started running, I asked Tom how far we would be going. He said, "How about around the island?" Around the island? You gotta be kidding me, I thought to myself. I couldn't let this old man outrun me, so I said, "Sure, let's do

it." Ten miles later, in complete
exhaustion and silent humiliation,
I finished the Tybee Island run.

> " Pick a BHAG goal. "

"Pick a BHAG goal," Tom said. "Big, Hairy, Audacious Goal." Okay, how about a half marathon? I signed up for the Detroit Free-Press Half Marathon, and started to train.

What to do about my "Emotional" area goals? I rated this area a little low because I knew that I had problems with worry and sometimes anxiety. Nothing that I thought was serious, but I knew I could improve here. I had been to counseling a couple of times over the past twenty years, when I felt stress at work and at home building, and had trouble coping. I usually found help in one or two sessions, and then moved on feeling much better. The volatility of my new recruiting business offered new reasons to worry, but luckily we were doing well enough that the worry sessions didn't last too long. I did recognize that if I could minimize my worry and anxiety, and focus more on the present work, I'd perform better in my new role. Following my new-found love of reading, I knew that I could improve in any area of my life if I read the right books.

For some reason, I remembered a little book I read back in college. Other than textbooks, I never read in college. I don't remember why I even had this book, and I know I didn't go out and buy it. I never bought books. Paying for all of my college through student loans, I was absolutely broke. With no spending money, I donated (sold) plasma twice per week at the local Red Cross. Twenty dollars per week for giving blood, and for a good cause, what a deal! A few months later, my arms started to look like I was a drug addict. I used the twenty dollars for beer, not drugs. Oh, the book. It was called *Gifts from Eykis*, and written by some guy named Wayne Dyer.

This little paperback told a fictitious story in such a profound way that it changed me. It laid out the very useless nature of the emotions of worry and regret, and yet I somehow, while profoundly impacted by the book, put those lessons away, into the rear filing cabinet of my brain. Twenty five years later, I recalled that book, bought a new copy from Amazon, reread it, and loved it. I then started voraciously reading other books written by Wayne Dyer and Eckhart Tolle, and recognized that my amount of worry and anxiety both reduced dramatically as my spiritual growth accelerated. The many references in the Bible about faith versus fear were starting to make sense, and I recognized as I learned to control my thinking and stay more in the present moment, growth in all areas of my life began to accelerate.

The areas of "Financial" and "Relationships" were both, I thought, in very good shape. My work in these areas was simply to keep on keeping on—maintaining already good momentum.

I would soon find out that I was not seeing these areas as clearly as I should, as major changes were just around the corner.

Chapter Four: Derailed

"Honey, I love you, but there's something I need to say to you," Carol calmly stated as I washed the dishes after dinner. She was a phenomenal cook, and over the years we had somehow settled into a routine where she bought the groceries and cooked the meals, and I did the dishes. No doubt I was the big winner with that agreement.

"Okay, what's up," I said. Carol told me that she wanted us to move back to Nashville. Patrick was now a senior in high school, and after he graduated, she wanted to settle back into her beloved Tennessee. Dana was doing great at Auburn University, and Ellen was married and settled in Dallas working in a marketing role. Carol said that we had moved too many times, and she wanted this to be her final move. She stated that I could do my business anywhere, and before I got the company too settled into the Michigan scene, it would be best if we went ahead and moved and put in roots in the Nashville area. Carol's comment was much more of a statement than a request. I certainly wasn't expecting this, and it took a few minutes for the idea to settle in. In my typical fashion, I said, "Okay, we'll move back to Nashville." I had just opened the recruiting business six months earlier. My initial success was very good, but I was worried about the disruption of moving my business this soon. The majority of our clients were in the

Detroit area, and all of my professional experience had been in automotive manufacturing. Would I be able to continue the business living in Nashville? After saying, "Okay," my mind started working on all the things to be done to make this move actually happen.

Carol was excited about the idea of moving back to Tennessee. She told everyone, and started to reconnect with Nashville friends. She wanted to get a one-story house out in the country, with a big front porch, and some rocking chairs, like the ones you see at Cracker Barrel. She couldn't wait to get to the point to where we could both rock in those chairs, drink wine, play with the five dogs, and enjoy retirement. Retirement? You've got to be kidding me! I couldn't believe what she was saying. I was only 47, just starting my new business, and my head was full of new ideas, new goals, and new ways of thinking about the future. There was no part of me that wanted to retire. Absolutely none. How in the world would I pay for things? Did she think we were made of money? The word "retire" made me sad. I had seen so many people work full careers in jobs that they hated, only to save a little bit of money and make it to retirement, to then either be miserable or die. This was not the future I wanted.

I didn't argue with her—just stayed quiet and went along with the plan. We took a couple of house-hunting trips to the Nashville area, and ultimately bought a home, on five acres, nestled between two large farms in rural Christiana, Tennessee. I negotiated the option to transfer my recruiting business franchise from Michigan to Murfreesboro, Tennessee, and paid a huge sum of money to exercise that option. I didn't want to move to Tennessee, but I didn't share those thoughts with anyone. While I loved living in the Nashville area before, actually this would the third time, I knew that there is no "going back" in life. I also loved living in San Antonio. I loved living in Columbia, Missouri. I loved living in Tokyo. I could see that Carol's desire was to return to the healthy, happy life that she lived in Nashville some ten years earlier. She hated life in Michigan, almost as much as she hated life in Texas. I had liked every place where we had lived. I realized that I measured my happiness mostly on the quality of the relationships in my life, and not on the physical place, the house, the traffic or the weather. We simply viewed these things differently.

Goal-setting was starting to become a habit. Having constructed a fairly elaborate goal-tracking system in Microsoft Excel, I would update my status on a monthly basis prior to my coaching calls with Tom Hill. My goals were organized according to the six priority areas of my life, and specific targets were set for six year, three year, 18-month and 90-day time frames. I color-coded each area: green for complete or on track, yellow for falling behind, and red for trouble or no meaningful action or progress.

It was Friday night. I was enjoying a cold Bud Light, sitting at the desk in our study. It was starting to get dark outside, and I was feeling peaceful having wrapped up a great week at work. Our study was previously the tiny master bedroom for the prior owners of the house on Pounds Court. When we bought this house, which was clearly too small for the four of us, we immediately had a large master bedroom suite added on to the back. This resulted in turning the old master bedroom into a funky little study that you had to walk through to get to the master. I had just closed another big recruiting project that afternoon, and was feeling great about the future. With a coaching call with Tom Hill scheduled for the upcoming Monday morning, I knew I should update my goals, and think about setting some new ones.

Spiritual: I'm getting better at daily Bible reading and honest prayers. Leading the youth group at church has been wonderful. We're doing a Habitat for Humanity project in a few weeks. I think I'm feeling closer to God.

Physical: I've signed up for the Detroit Half Marathon next fall. This seems crazy, and I don't know if I can actually do it, but Tom will agree that it's a nice BHAG goal.

Relationships: I'm starting to initiate professional relationships with more people, following Tom's networking system. All is great with Carol and the kids.

Emotional: I'm reading *The Power of Intention* by Wayne Dyer. An amazing book and it's really affecting me.

Intellectual and Professional: I'm learning to read faster through the EyeQ lessons. I've also started tracking the books that I'm reading, and am now re-reading *Synchronicity* by Joseph Jaworski.

Financial: This area is looking great, and I can't wait to tell Tom how I'm doing. I think I'll be able to pay off the credit cards and start making extra payments on the mortgage. The idea of being debt-free and having complete financial freedom is starting to resonate with me. I realize that the Audi payment will be around for a while, and I'm a little worried about how long it will take to sell the house at Pounds Court once we move to Nashville.

I heard her coming around the corner. Quickly minimizing the computer screen, I went back to browsing the day's news on AOL. Carol quietly brushed past me into the master bathroom, and I reopened my goal tracking Excel sheet. What new goals should I set? I wondered what Tom would think about these goals, and about how I'm doing overall. He always told me to reach for more, and that I'm not dreaming big enough. I started to type and heard the bathroom door open. Quickly, I hid the Excel sheet again and returned to AOL.

"What are you doing?" she said.

"Nothing—just reading the news."

"What were you just looking at? I saw you change the screen when I came into the room."

"Um, nothing really," I replied.

Squeezing my shoulder blades as she looked over my back, "Are you looking at porn?" she asked.

"Oh my God!" I said. "You gotta be kidding me—of course not! Look, I'm just updating my goals."

Carol cocked her head as she studied the grid lines of detail on my elaborate color-coded spreadsheet. "Your goals? On a Friday night? You gotta be kidding me! Porn would have been better. You're such a nerd," she muttered out as she quickly strode back into the kitchen.

It was getting dark outside, and the sun was setting as I looked outside the window behind my desk and over the computer screen. I sat there in silence, feeling numb, and stunned. The room started to tilt and I felt out of balance. I couldn't catch my breath. I sat there alone and quietly observed myself, trying to make sense of what just happened. I felt trapped and confused. I think she was joking, or was she? I'm pretty thick-skinned, and my feelings aren't hurt all that easily. But this was somehow different. I felt the sense of a sharp knife stabbing deep into my heart, into my soul. Carol thought it was silly that I was writing down my goals. I was getting energized from doing it—feeling a sense of purpose and connection to something real that I hadn't felt in a long, long time. I felt tugged in two different directions: continuing on the well-worn path of husband, father, worker, bread-winner, dutiful follower, or on a new path of growth and passion and connection to something bigger and more meaningful.

"Dinner's ready," she called as she set the kitchen table.

"Be right there." I saved the Excel file, turned off the computer and desk lamp, and shuffled into the kitchen. Carol had cooked her famous barbecue meatloaf, along with mashed potatoes—my favorite dinner of all time. Two glasses of chardonnay were poured. I sat, at my usual spot, hungry but somehow without appetite. Going through the motions, I chewed my food, recognizing that my taste buds were not working. After doing the dishes, I joined Carol in the living room while she and the five dogs nestled on the couch to watch a DVR'd episode of *American Idol*.

Everything was going well, except for the relationship with Carol. I noticed that as I came home from work with excitement of new deals, new ideas, new challenges—she would quickly change the subject. It seemed strange to me that she wasn't as turned on as I was, and as my energy built, I felt her energy, especially for me, wilt. Our intimacy, which previously was strong and steady, started to drift for the first time in our marriage. As Patrick's high school graduation date grew nearer, Carol and I drifted further apart. Her future was aimed directly at a comfortable retirement in Tennessee; my future was in a different direction—to grow, to stretch, to achieve and to do more.

Having signed up for the Detroit Free Press Half Marathon to take place in mid-October, it was time to start training. Following the Hal Higdon Novice Half Marathon Training Guide, I began running outside four to five times per week. Carol was adamantly against my goal of running such a long distance, stating that it would certainly damage my knees and cripple me for the future. She demanded that I stop. Uncharacteristically, I told her that I was going to continue. As the required training runs got longer and longer, taking up more and more time, the tension between Carol and I grew. During one heated argument, Carol asked, "What are you running from?"

My response was, "I'm not running from anything. I just want to get in shape for the half marathon." She shook her head in disgust.

We moved to Christiana, Tennessee on August 1st. We had not sold the house in Michigan, and Patrick decided to live there while he went to college at nearby Washtenaw Community College. This was ideal for us as he could keep the house ready for showings, which we hoped would happen anytime. Tension between Carol and I grew every day in our new home in Tennessee. I couldn't let go of my excitement and energy to grow my business and my life, and Carol couldn't let go of her desire to retire. We had completely and literally opposite views of the future. After one week, a major fight erupted, and Carol told me to leave. We had been married twenty years. We hardly ever fought, and had what most people thought was the perfect marriage. We had always put the other one first. We had date night weekly. We had a great family. We had never before had any serious marital problems, had never separated or gone to counseling. Sure, Carol had her years of serious health issues, but the marriage had stayed strong. I didn't understand what was going on now, but it was clear that we were at a crossroads.

I quickly loaded up my truck with my clothes and office stuff, and drove eight hours back to the yellow house on Pounds Court in Michigan. I called Patrick about two hours into the drive, and tearfully told him what was going on. I was amazed and proud of how mature and supportive he was in his response.

Once back in Michigan, I went back to work in our

office in Howell, and found a therapist. The counselor was a female Christian marriage counselor, who came strongly recommended by several friends whom she helped in strengthening their marriages. I had great hopes that she would do the same for mine. After several tearful visits, she advised that I should divorce Carol. I couldn't believe what I was hearing, but as I painfully peeled back the layers of my life and our long marriage, a new picture was evolving of the true nature of our relationship. During therapy, I learned about codependency, and reluctantly realized that I was severely codependent in my relationship with Carol. Early in our dating relationship and throughout our marriage, Carol and I had an agreement that went, "If I always put you first, and you always put me first, we will have the perfect marriage." So, that's what I did—literally. Every decision I made was based on my perception of what does she need, what would she think, and at the core—what would she think of me. As I lived my life always putting her first, with little to no regard for what I needed or what I would like to do, my batteries ran dry as my frustration ran high.

Through months of ongoing counseling, I learned that it is my obligation to put myself first. I learned that being independent, as opposed to codependent, and through focusing and investing in my own health and growth, I would be a much better person and therefore a much better partner. Carol wanted no part in this way of thinking.

My therapist surprised me by recommending that I read *Jonathan Livingston Seagull* by Richard Bach. This simple children's book opened my eyes to the possibility of living my unique life, independent of the opinions of other people. A life with growth and authenticity forever unfolding into the future. This book also rekindled a passion I had for flying, and

I quickly started taking flight lessons at the nearby Howell airport. Twice each week at the crack of dawn, I along with my flight instructor, would walk around the Cessna 152 to conduct the pre-flight inspection, go through the checklist prior to taxi and takeoff, and I would enjoy the sheer thrill of taking off, flying and repeatedly landing that small plane. A very expensive new hobby, I was addicted to the excitement of being in flight, and I was also tasting the fruit of my new freedom, being able to do something just because I wanted to, and because I could.

I met with my business lawyer and soon filed for divorce. As the papers were served in Tennessee, an earthquake of emotion and strong reaction from family and friends hit from all directions. My only explanation to others was that I had reached a fork in the road where I had to make a decision. My option became stay with Carol and shut down any possibility for personal and professional growth, or divorce and be free to grow—quite possibly being single, alone and losing the love and respect of my children, friends and other family.

As I pondered the path of no growth, it felt as if the air was sucked out of my lungs. I had moments of feeling that if I was not free to grow, I would die. But I was not thinking about suicide, and I was not depressed. I simply felt that if I could not grow, I would suffocate.

Carol was completely against the idea of divorce. She had been divorced before, and made it clear to me that she wanted no part of being a divorced woman. She, as well as many other family members and friends, thought that something was medically wrong with me. Most thought that at a minimum I had experienced a mid-life crisis. Other theories were that I had suffered an aneurism, had fallen and hit my head, had narcissistic personality disorder, and had either an affair or was secretly homosexual. As each of these theories were thrown out at me, my resolve to focus on my future, on my growth, and on my authentic path in life strengthened.

Living alone was strange and uncomfortable. Weekly therapy, life coaching, my work, running, flight lessons, and a new-found love for books and reading were what got me though this very difficult time. As I had bouts of trouble falling asleep, or staying asleep at night, I was relieved when I discovered the books on my nightstand fought off the insomnia. I learned to love the opportunity to read and it didn't matter what time of night it was.

During our separation, communications with Carol were extremely tense and adversarial. She threatened to sue my therapist for malpractice, she wrote a letter to my attorney asking him to have me admitted into psychiatric care, and she wrote Tom a long letter blaming him for ruining our marriage. With lawyers involved on both sides, the fight and the costs escalated each week.

I ran the Detroit Half Marathon. Just over 13 grueling miles in two hours, gray sky on even grayer pavement. My feet and legs were on fire in spite of the frigid temperatures. Forgetting to bring my headphones, I was forced to run the race without music. I trained while listening to music, typically Christian music, which saved me from my lizard brain trying to outthink the many problems in my life. Finishing the race, where there were 20,000 other runners, I found myself completely alone and broken. My entire body ached. My heart ached and I was physically in pain as I pondered the condition of my life. I had never before experienced such sadness, such aloneness, such emptiness. There was no one there to cheer me on, no one there to congratulate me when I crossed the finish line. Hobbling for an hour like a crippled old man, I tried to find where I had parked my truck in the ruins of downtown Detroit. After a one-hour drive home to Pounds Court, I collapsed in physical and emotional exhaustion.

I loved leading the All Saints Lutheran Church high school youth group. In addition to weekly meetings in the basement of the parish house, we also had monthly outings as a group to visit and learn about different religions. I think I learned more than the students, and I thoroughly enjoyed each of these visits. After attending services at a Buddhist monastery, a Mormon service, and an Islamic mosque, our group scheduled a visit to a local synagogue. We had no idea that we would be attending an actual bar mitzvah. During this sacred ceremony, which was attended by several hundred people, including the dozen of us from the Lutheran church, I was overcome with the sense of history, of family, of honor. As I watched the 13-year-old boy read from the Torah, with his father, uncles, grandfather and great-grandfather all laying their hands on him, I felt the presence of God. I also felt God saying to me, "Brett, you are a wimp. Don't give up on your marriage—on your family. Go back to Carol and put your marriage back together." I wept.

As the Saturday afternoon ceremony at the synagogue took much longer than I had planned, I realized that I was going to be late for a meeting with my accountant to discuss the valuation of my recruiting business as it related to the property settlement. As part of the divorce, Carol would be awarded one-half of the value of all our assets, including my business. I called the accountant and he agreed to stay late to see me.

The meeting was short. He shared the good news first. Given my business is only viable if I am working in it; it has basically no financial value as an entity by itself. Then he shared the bad news. He had already talked with Carol's attorney and their valuation had the business worth a great deal of money. To resolve the difference, I learned that the judge would simply split the difference in valuations, and I would be required to pay Carol one-half of that amount. I did not have this much money. The only other alternative was to sell or close the business.

When I returned home to cold and empty Pounds Court, I was drained yet flooded with emotion. Did God really speak to me at that synagogue? Was that a sign that I should reverse course on this divorce? Am I doing the right thing? In a split second of what felt like pure clarity, I picked up my cell phone and called Carol. She answered. She sounded unusually happy, like she had been laughing. I told her that I had been thinking about things, and that I'd like to talk about getting back together. She said that she would like to try as well. Feeling an overwhelming sense of relief and peace, I sensed the love returning in our relationship. We decided that it would be fun to have a date weekend back in Nashville, and if things went well, we could discuss moving back together. Two weeks later, after talking on the phone daily and rekindling our mutual attraction, we spent a romantic weekend in Tennessee. Returning back to Brighton, I met with my attorney and terminated the divorce proceedings. I soon loaded up my truck, with my clothes and office stuff, and drove back to Christiana, Tennessee.

Christmas in Tennessee, reunited with Carol and the entire family, was wonderful. I loved being around family and friends, and thoroughly enjoyed the holidays. Carol agreed to be supportive of my new goals, and I agreed to support her as well. We decided to start marriage counseling right after the New Year, as we both wanted to rebuild our foundation and get back to the great marriage that we had before.

But the renewed marriage quickly started to unravel. A

guy that Carol had dated during our separation continued to send her text messages. Even though Carol and I were now back together, she asked me if it would be okay if they stayed friends. Carol also started taking classes to be a bartender, telling me that she needed this as a backup career if I left her again. During our counseling sessions, Carol refused to do the couples' homework, and told our counselor that I was the one that needed to be fixed, not her, nor the marriage. It soon became clear that neither Carol nor I were open to compromise on our distinctly different views of the future. After several meetings, the counseling sessions fell apart. For the second time, a therapist advised that I should proceed with divorce. After two months of escalating arguments, I moved out again—this time to a small apartment near Murfreesboro, Tennessee, about seven miles from Carol.

Having now officially moved the recruiting business to Tennessee, I set about establishing my new life there. I attended a large non-denominational Christian church, and loved it. I went to a divorce support group called Divorce Care. I registered for the Nashville Marathon, trained well and finished the 26-mile run in just over five hours. Tom Hill ran the same half marathon, and Dana and her boyfriend, Lee, were there at the finish line to congratulate me. It was a beautiful day, and I felt a huge sense of accomplishment that I had tackled such a big goal. Running was becoming an important part of my life, and I looked forward to the next event.

In the summer of 2009 the national economy was in the tank. The automotive industry, in which most of my recruiting business still resided, was in a huge depression. My house on Pounds Court, now completely empty as Patrick had moved to an apartment near his college, had lost half of its value. The monthly costs of supporting Carol, the Michigan house, my apartment and struggling business were eating up what was left of our savings.

To hold myself together, to have hope for the future, I was reading, running, praying, meditating, attending yoga classes, and working. I knew that I needed to do the work to learn to be happy, truly happy, while living alone. I viewed this time in my life, and the process ahead of me, as if I were about to walk alone across a vast desert. In my mind's eye, I could see the agony of the journey ahead for me, but knew that on the other side, a great life was there to be lived. I also knew that I needed to rebuild my independence and identity before I would be healthy enough to be in another marriage, if ever.

The divorce was final on September 11, 2009. In early October I loaded up my pickup truck with my clothes and my office stuff, and drove eight hours back to the cold, empty house on Pounds Court. During the property settlement phase of the divorce proceedings, I didn't want to fight, and I didn't want to drag things out. I didn't want the kids to be pulled into it, and I didn't want Carol to be a financial burden for them. This was my problem, not theirs. I wanted to maintain control of my business. I didn't care about material things. I wanted to be able to be free to pursue my dreams—to be able to breathe.

I gave up half of our assets and agreed to lifetime alimony. This meant that Carol would never need to work. My lawyer told me that I was crazy. Maybe I was, but it felt right to me. I took on the full financial burden of another household for which I would have no interaction, and in return, I gained the precious freedom to be able to breathe deeply, and the freedom to live my authentic life.

Chapter Five: Flying Solo

Home alone. Uncomfortable. Too much time to think about things—random things and sad things. Not many happy things. Maybe this is what divorce is supposed to feel like. I'm lonely and I don't like living alone. I know that's not healthy. I know that I have to get to the point that I'm happy, truly happy, being alone. I'm realizing that I have so much to do in rebuilding myself. I'm learning how so much of my previous twenty years was on autopilot, heading to a destination that I had not set. The Eagle Scout in me found two decades of meaning and happiness in being the provider and the follower. I was proud to carry that burden, and proud of the family that I supported and loved. I never once, not even in a whisper, thought that I had a bad marriage or was on the wrong track in life. I buried those feelings so deep that I didn't even know they were there. How could I have deceived myself for so long?

> Maybe now is my time to dedicate myself to becoming the very best person I can be.

This new path that I've chosen sure feels right to me, but my life in the past felt right as well. Am I lying to myself now? How do I know what is right?

* * *

Goals. Set goals and do the work to achieve them. Set goals for all areas of my life, not just in making money. Tom has told me that, "One person, attracted to me because of who I have become, can change my life forever." Maybe now is my time to dedicate myself to becoming the very best person I can be, and maybe, just maybe, I'll attract that perfect one person.

I started attending The River, a growing non-denominational Christian church in Brighton. I loved the energy of this church, along with the music, the message and the teaching of the senior pastor. I found my Bible in the few belongings that I moved back to Michigan with me, and started reading from the New Testament every morning. I felt my connection to God growing and my interest in the church growing as well.

The economy in Michigan was now completely in the toilet. General Motors had declared bankruptcy, and Chrysler was taken over by Fiat. Ford was the only U.S. automaker that did not take bailout money from the federal government. Automotive suppliers were dropping like flies. No one was hiring. My little recruiting company was now just two and one-half years old, and we were barely making it. Was I going to be one of those small businesses that don't survive three years? I had two choices: go back to work for another company, or do everything I could to make the recruiting company survive. I chose option number two, and decided to put all I could into saving my little company.

Goals. I've been taught to set goals in all areas of my life, not just on money. Balance—I've been taught to pursue balance. How is my balance? In my last coaching call, Tom asked me this same question, and my answers were:

Spiritual: 7 —Feeling guilt about the divorce and impact on Carol and the kids. Wondering how this all plays in God's eyes.

Physical: 8 —My new love of running has held me through some tough times.

Relationships: 2 —The lowest of all lows. Not much to brag about here.

Emotional: 5 —The guilt and regret continue to nag at me.

Intellectual: 7 —Learning more about sales and business leadership.

Financial: 4 —Business struggling while expenses are staggering.

My Circle of Life now looked like this:

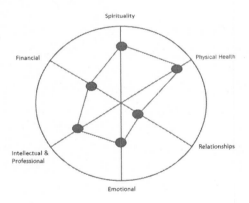

Wow ... my life has sure taken a turn for the worse since I first drew this picture. What am I doing to myself? While sad, I knew. I knew that I was purging myself and creating a blank canvas from which to design and create my authentic life. The areas which were low were the areas where I needed to do the work. Work does not scare me, and I felt ready to tackle it all.

Feeling good about my new church home and my spiritual growth, I moved to "Physical." I was loving my new running habit, and signed up for another half marathon. I also joined the Brighton fitness center and added weight lifting twice per week.

"Relationships." Whew ... where to start? The main thing tugging at me was how to rebuild the relationships with my three kids. My goal—to love them unconditionally and allow them each as much time as they needed to come around.

> " I found that my problems seemed to dim when I did work to help other people. "

What about professional relationships? I had several friends in the Detroit area, but not many in Brighton. I decided to check out the local Rotary Club, and after attending a few meetings as a guest, I was invited to join, which I did. I loved the good works that the Rotary Club did in the area, and found that my problems seemed to dim when I did work to help other people. This was a lesson I would relearn over and over in the coming years.

Tom suggested I look for a Toastmasters Club. This would be a great way to improve in my speaking and communications skills in general, but would also be a way to meet some new people. A Google search for a local Toastmasters group showed one that met weekly at a local business called The Insights Group hosted by a lady named Sandi Maki. I emailed Sandi about the group, and she immediately responded by inviting me to the meeting the following evening, and closed her email message with her standard, "Hugs, Sandi." My heart was warmed by an email from a lady I didn't know who just gave me a virtual hug.

At the meeting, I was greeted with a real hug from Sandi, and also a hearty handshake from her business partner, Al Curtis. Sandi and Al were the co-sponsors for the weekly Toastmasters group, meeting at their "entrepreneurs' clubhouse," the Insights Group. Twelve other people were at the meeting and after some introductions and standard Toastmasters protocol,

Sandi asked me to come up to the front of the room and give a speech about myself. She grinned as I meekly stood up, and somehow gave a speech for which I had no preparation. I didn't remember much of what I said, but found confidence in the fact that I was able to give an impromptu speech in front of a bunch of people whom I didn't know. As I looked over at Sandi after I was done with the short speech, she discreetly winked at me with a look of "job well done."

I went home that evening to my empty house with a new feeling of hope and confidence—both in my ability to speak in public, but more importantly in my ability to make new friends in my brave new world.

Al and Sandi have since become very, very good friends, and they have been instrumental in my personal and professional growth over the past six years. In addition to encouraging my growth as a public speaker, they have also been key to my understanding of social media and in my growth and capabilities as a marketer as well as a life coach.

The remaining missing piece in my relationship puzzle was the lack of a romantic partner. I wanted a girlfriend. I knew it was probably too soon to start dating, and the divorce support group at church had even suggested that I wait one full year for every five years that I had been married. I was married for twenty years! There was no way, absolutely no way that I was going to wait four years before I went on a date!

I was new to Facebook. I had set up my Facebook account and created a profile a few months earlier. I found this to be a great way to keep up with what's going on in other people's lives, especially my kids and other family members. While walking around the big front pasture at Pounds Court one cold, starlit night, my cell phone buzzed. I looked at it and saw the notification of a new Facebook friend request. Looking closer, I saw that Amy Jones, a girl I had dated in high school, had asked to "friend" me. My breath was taken away. My mind immediately returned to those times with Amy back in high school. I could remember her perfume and the softness of her lips. I could remember her giggle and that cute smile she used when she flirted with me. I remembered the special times when we were alone in the dark. I also remembered how much I liked her mom and dad. We had broken up when I went off to college, as I was two years older than her, and didn't want to be tied down at school. She later went on to marry one of the other guys from our high school, had several children, and I had lost touch with her.

I responded to her friend request, and we soon found each other on the phone for hours, catching up on lost time. Her voice was identical to the cute, girly voice I remembered from thirty years prior. As my memories of Amy sharpened, the mutual flirtation and passion built with each call. I learned that she was divorced; she learned that I was divorced, and we quickly arranged for a weekend reunion.

This is how it works! I've heard lots of stories about high school flames being reunited later in life, and I was ecstatic that this was now happening to me. Wait four years? Nope— not going to do it! Amy is the one, and I can't wait to be back in her arms.

After an 11-hour drive back to Missouri, I walked up the steps to her front door. I hardly recognized the person who came to greet me, and I'm guessing that she barely recognized me as well. I wanted this to work, but I didn't feel a connection to this person.

Our memories were real, but the present was not what either thought it would be. After an awkward weekend together, I sheepishly drove back to Michigan, feeling terrible about how

I might have hurt this sweet lady, but also learning a huge life lesson. You can't go back. I was no longer 18 years young, and never will be again. Amy was no longer 16 years young, and will also never be there again. Over the thirty years apart, we had become completely different people, and there was now no spark or compatibility.

Wait! I'm a recruiter. This will be easy. I'll use technology. I signed up for Match.com, and eHarmony. My computer screen was filled with potential dates. I thought that, at 48 years old, it may be tough to get a date. Boy, was I wrong. I quickly realized that there are thousands of women out there in their forties who are looking for a guy. The problem, I was not attracted to the great majority of them. I knew what I wanted, and I was in no mood to settle. I thought my list was simple: no smokers, must be shorter than me, preferably athletic, have a job, be cheerful and optimistic, and be pretty. I didn't think this short list of criteria was all that picky, but I soon found out that it eliminated most of the ladies on the market. I went on a few dates, but none worked out.

Frustrated, I shut down my Match and eHarmony accounts, deciding to focus all of my time and energy on other parts of my life. Continuing to grow in my relationships in the local community, as well as my professional relationships with clients and people in the Tom Hill network, my life was buzzing with activity. Who needs a girlfriend anyway?

Life is strange and unpredictable. This is a truth that I've witnessed over and over. In one week, I was approached by three different friends who had friends of theirs that they wanted to set me up with. I get it. This is how it works. It's when you are not looking that the right person will come your way. I've heard that several times before, but I never believed it, and I'm too action-oriented to just sit around and wait for the right person to come my way. Now, this crazy saying is maybe coming true for me.

I agreed to blind dates with each of these three ladies, one per week over the next three weeks. Dates number one and number two were absolute nightmares. Without going into any details, I can simply say that my friends had NO IDEA OF WHAT I WAS LOOKING FOR! I was honestly amazed at how completely off the mark these two dates were for me, and I politely shared with my friends that I guess I was super picky, and also something about not being quite ready to date—a little white lie.

But then date number three was actually a good match, and we ended up dating for several months. Complications of her children, her ex-husband, demands of her career and my career, as well as miscommunication on Facebook ultimately caused that relationship to sputter out.

I was drained, and decided again to stop the pursuit of Ms. Right.

I then met a real-life matchmaker at a party in Detroit. At this same party, I met several couples who had married through this matchmaker-lady, and a few other people who were dating people she had connected to them. After a subsequent meeting at her office, and after going through an exhaustive profiling process, I hired her to be my personal matchmaker. Expensive, but hopefully worth the cost. After a few dates with different women, and adjusting our collective knowledge of what I liked and didn't like, I finally met a great woman, and we started dating.

Business continued to be a struggle. Not able to pay all of my bills, including alimony, I was dipping into savings each month. Trying my best to keep my chin up, I did the work each day to market for new search assignments, as well as manage the recruiters working in the firm, including now my son, Patrick. Patrick worked part-time while he was pursuing his degree at Washtenaw.

Tom Hill, always there to help me, suggested I meet with a very successful sales trainer and recruiter in St. Louis. Tom Schaff had built a very successful business in training sales professionals for major corporations all across the country, and as part of his business, he would often be asked to recruit for experienced sales people. Tom and I met at a coffee shop in St. Louis, and had a great discussion about the possibility of collaborating on future recruiting projects. As part of getting to know each other, Tom asked if I was open to taking two online assessments that he gives to the salespeople he trains. This would allow me to have a first-hand look at these tools as a recruiting aid, and give Tom a sense of my strengths and weaknesses as a sales professional.

Three weeks later, I was back in Michigan at a coffee shop on a cold, dreary Saturday morning. Drinking a latte, I opened my laptop and downloaded the day's email messages. I saw the message from Tom Schaff with two attachments. After downloading the pdf files, I began to read the results. My heart sank. On both assessments, the result was clear that I was not the right profile to be in a sales profession. One report even stated, in bold red letters, that if I were an applicant for a sales role, that I should not be hired, and that I was not trainable.

The room started to tilt. I looked around in a daze. I reread the report, and it still said the same thing. My blood was boiling as I absorbed what I had just read. What do you mean, I should not be hired in a sale role? My entire business relies on my abilities as a salesperson. I've been in the top 10 offices of SRA for the past two years, and won the award for new office of the year in 2008. I'm a very good salesperson! I was pissed, and could not believe what I was reading. As I returned to the email message from Tom Schaff, I read where he wrote, "Brett, please take a look at the attached assessments. Given these results, I'd suggest we not collaborate on recruiting projects at this time. Also, you may consider going to Sandler Sales Training."

That jerk! I spent my money to fly all the way to St. Louis to meet this guy and to hear this? Three deep breaths and my mind was spinning as I stared out the window, pondering what to do next. Pissed off, I closed my laptop and went home.

In my next coaching call with Tom Hill, I shared with him the extent to which my business was suffering. The line of credit at the bank was almost gone, and I had borrowed money from my life insurance policy to make the last payroll. The recruiting projects that our team was currently working on were all contingency-type versus retained. With contingency recruiting projects, a fee is only collected if and when someone is hired. Companies often times start contingency searches with no real commitment to making a hire, and they also at times use multiple recruiters on the same project. With retained searches, companies pay recruiters some money up front, and then work with the recruiter until the right candidate is found and hired. Our closing rate was around 12 percent, meaning that we would make money on only one of eight recruiting projects that we started. I knew that the retained search model had a much higher closing percentage, but had no idea about how to acquire retained business. This was an exhausting reality, and a treadmill that I wanted to get off of.

"Brett, how about let's set up a Hill's Angel Action Board," Tom Hill said during our next coaching call.

"What's an Action Board?" I replied.

"We can get several of the Hill's Angels together to come

visit you, listen and diagnose what's going on in your business, and then give you advice," Tom said.

I learned that several of the forty-some Hill's Angels had been part of similar interventions in the past, and that they had been very helpful in turning some businesses around. Tom was sure that he could get some of his Hill's Angels to volunteer to help me, all at no cost to me, and he asked who I would like. After some discussion, we agreed that a group made up of Craig Hughes, Bob Doig, Dick Burke and Britt Hunt would be ideal. Tom did his magic, and to my complete surprise, all four of these guys agreed to fly to Detroit and spend a couple of days meeting with me and my team at the Brighton office. Each of these men own and operate hugely successful businesses, and each are extremely busy. I was honored that these guys would spend their time and money to help me, and I was anxious to set up the meetings the best I could.

Borrowing office space from Al and Sandi's Insights Group, we spent two half-days dissecting my business, with breaks for lunch and a very nice dinner in downtown Brighton on the first evening. Going through the painstaking efforts to document the real history of the business to-date, the vulnerabilities and opportunities for improvement became clear.

During a visit to our offices, one of the gentlemen noticed on my wall a long sheet of paper, four feet tall, which listed each of the search projects that we had completed in the prior two plus years. We had just crossed the one-million dollar mark in revenue collected, and I was proud of that fact. When Dick asked me what this large piece of paper was for, I proudly shared that this was a visible record of each of the projects that we had completed, the name of each of the people that we had helped in landing a new job, and the money that we made for each project.

Dick asked again, "I understand what this is, but why do you have it on your wall? What does this have to do with anything about your business going forward?" Frustrated by his questions, I just shrugged it off as something he didn't understand.

As the Action Board intervention came to a conclusion, the full group met in our conference room for a recap. One by one, each of these super-successful businessmen gave me their honest opinions. While the recruiting business is worlds apart from the different businesses that these guys were running, I found value in each of the comments that were made. The most common suggestions were to improve in my sales-related efforts, and to broaden my client base and target markets. One of the gentlemen suggested that I go to Sandler Sales Training. As the comments went around the table, my friend and very successful entrepreneur from Nashville, Britt Hunt, stated in his unique Southern drawl, "Brett, I just don't think you have the passion to be successful in this business." He looked me straight in the eyes as he said this, without flinching. I was boiling inside, and wanted to get up right there and smack this guy in the face. I blankly stared back at him, and then looked at the floor.

After each of the gentlemen left and boarded their respective flights home, I went back to my quiet office to reflect upon what had just taken place. With over fifty specific recommendations made from the group, I had committed to documenting an action plan and sharing it, along with my progress, on a weekly basis to the full group. As I started to build my new Excel sheet, with a project called "Project Turnaround," my anger built again—both for the comments made about my "wallpaper" of completed search projects, and the stinging comment that I did not have the passion to succeed in my business.

Pushing back my chair, I went to my wall, pulled down the big sheet of paper, and wadded it into a huge paper ball. "Crap!" I yelled as I threw this sacred document of my scrawny business success into the trash can. "And, I'll show you," I said to myself as I remembered Britt Hunt's shark-eyed statement. "I'll show you all," I muttered as I turned out my office light and locked my door.

After a couple of beers at the Leaf, Barley and Vine wine shop across the street, I was finally calm enough to bear going home to my empty house. Did Britt Hunt say that to me to fire me up, or did he really believe it? Does he really think I don't have passion? I may not be the best sales guy or the best recruiter, but I absolutely know I have passion. And what was that comment from Dick Burke? Have I been spending too much of my energy reflecting on the past? Was my pride getting in my way? What if I really did convert that energy into planning and acting on plans for the future? My mind was starting to churn with new ideas, and I felt a renewal of energy and commitment. As humiliating as the process was, and in spite of getting angry and my feelings hurt, I could already see the growth that was taking place inside of me, and could anticipate the benefits that I would be seeing in my little business.

Chapter Six: Life can be Crunchy

After the intervention of the Hill's Angel group, I made several difficult but important changes at work, including letting a couple of employees go. That was tough. We also made a conscious decision to move the company culture from a "friends and family" business to a bon-a-fide enterprise where the customer and business performance comes first. Tightening up fairly loose five-year and one-year business plans, along with setting employee performance expectations and formal reviews were part of our new business culture. Being personally more focused on sales growth and less concerned about the day-to-day internal workings of the firm, I was experiencing new success in winning business in the fragile Detroit economy. I could see the turnaround in front of us, and I was excited to get the business on a growing, more profitable path. I was optimistic and energized.

* * *

My cell phone rang. Mom was in tears. "What's wrong?" I asked.

"The doctor told me that I may need a lung transplant," she sobbed. I couldn't believe what I was hearing. A what? I had never heard of a lung transplant. How in the world could they transplant a lung?

Over the past three decades, Mom and Dad had gone in different directions in life. Dad remarried soon after my parent's divorce, and he and my stepmother Pam had a child. After retiring from a full career with AT&T, Dad and Pam moved to Truman Lake, Missouri, where Pam has deep family ties. Dad has loved his retirement years, being close to family, the lake, and fishing. Unfortunately, a lifetime of smoking finally caught up with him, and he now struggles with breathing challenges caused by COPD.

Mom also had breathing issues. Hers were most likely the result a lifetime of smoking, coupled with the side effects of chemotherapy and radiation treatments from fighting breast cancer ten years earlier. This was the same year that Mom lost her second husband, John, to a heart attack. My little sister Tracey also fought the same breast cancer at the same time as Mom, but sadly Tracey eventually died of the dreaded disease. Mom won her fight over cancer, but had been struggling with her breathing for the past several years. Having been on continuous oxygen for the past two, family and friends had quietly become accustomed to this as her new normal. My brother Mark and I had settled into a false belief that she would live this way for a long, long time. She was tough as nails, and had been through an incredibly amount of adversity in her life. We knew that she could handle anything.

Over the past several months, Mom's breathing deteriorated significantly. Concerned by this development, her pulmonologist near her home in Florida suggested that she look into the Duke Lung Transplant Program in Durham, North Carolina. Duke was known for having one of the country's best lung transplant programs. The first step would be for Mom to go to Durham for a week-long series of tests, evaluations, and meetings with specialists and surgeons. The great news—one of Mom's very best friends from previous days when she lived in Dallas now lived in nearby Cary, North Carolina, and Norma offered to help Mom through the week. Mom, Mark and I were all nervous about what was to come, but happy that Mom's friend would be there with her.

Five days before her trip to Durham, Mom got a call from Norma, and learned that she would not be able to help her at Duke. After reading through the staggering deck of paperwork that Duke Hospital required her to sign, which outlined the responsibilities of being a caregiver for this important week, my mom's friend backed out. Norma was also helping her own daughter and grandchildren, and didn't think that she could also be Mom's caregiver during this critical time. Mom called me again in tears.

"Stop crying," I said. "I'll go with you."

My brother's wife, Gretchen, drove Mom 12 hours up from Niceville, Florida, and I flew into the Raleigh-Durham airport from Detroit. I've traveled a lot in my life and previous career, but never to the Raleigh-Durham area, which is also called "The Triangle," in honor of Raleigh, Durham and Chapel Hill. Gretchen flew back home, and for the following week, I accompanied Mom daily to different parts of the sprawling Duke Hospital system for what seemed like endless tests. We soon found out that she had a disease called idiopathic pulmonary fibrosis. Idiopathic is a big word for "no one has any idea for what causes this disease." On Thursday of that week, Mom went through a fairly invasive test called a heart catheterization, to check out the strength and status of her heart. To be accepted as a lung transplant recipient, the surgeons want to make sure that the patient will not suffer a stroke, heart attack, or any other fatal problem during or immediately after the surgery.

Friday was a big day, for which we both had a lot of hope *and* anxiety. We would be meeting with the world-renowned surgeon who had helped make the Duke Lung Transplant Program so successful. Dr. Davis, late to the appointment, without emotion or care, told Mom that she was too fat, too weak, too old, and that he didn't know if she would survive the transplant surgery, if she was lucky enough to have one. It was also clear that her lung function was deteriorating quickly, and the doctors didn't know how much longer she would survive without a transplant. They told her that she should go home, and they'd get back to her within a few weeks on their decision.

Mom and I were both devastated. The prognosis seemed terrible. For the first time in my life, I started to think about how to handle things if Mom ended up dying. Next for us was a 12-hour drive home to Mom's house in Niceville. As part of the heart catheterization procedure, Mom was told that she could not fly for several days. Also, she was advised to stand and walk around every hour or so if she was going to be in a car for a long period of time. This was important to prevent blood clotting.

When we finally arrived at her house, Mom complained about numbness in her left leg. I was exhausted, and my left butt cheek was numb as well from sitting in the car all day. I said to Mom, "Just go to bed. We're both tired and we'll feel better in the morning." I left Mom at her house, drove to my brother's house nearby, and went to sleep.

"Brett, get up," Mark said as he knocked on the guest room door. "Mom called. It sounds like she had a stroke."

Jumping back into Mom's car, we sped back to her house. I told Mark about what Mom had said the evening before about her leg being numb. We rushed her to the local hospital, and yes, they soon diagnosed that she had suffered a stroke.

Pulling me aside in the hallway, the attending physician asked me when the symptoms first appeared. Sheepishly I responded, "Last night when we got home from driving from North Carolina."

"Last night?" the doctor said, as he glared at me "And you waited until this morning to bring her into the hospital? What were you thinking?"

I was thinking that I was an absolute loser. By this time, all of my brother's family and some other friends arrived at the hospital to check on Mom, and I left to go pick up lunch for the group. As I sat down in my mom's car, alone and feeling as low as I could ever remember, my glasses broke in half. They simply snapped into two pieces, both falling to the floorboard. I did not have a back-up pair with me, and I'm blind as a bat without glasses. Holding one lens with the broken frame and attached earpiece to my left eye, I clumsily drove around Destin trying to find a place that could fix my glasses, and also a place for lunch. "God, why is this happening," I uttered as I squinted through the wetness of both eyes. I was exhausted. I was confused. I was numb with dread and anxiety.

Two days later, I flew back to Detroit, and tried to refocus on work. Mom was still in the hospital in Florida, and thank God she was regaining her pre-stroke functionality. The tests revealed that she had suffered a TIA, a mini-stroke, and a full recovery was possible, but not guaranteed. Mark and his family were able to visit Mom at the hospital and help her with anything that she might need. I knew that even if she had a full recovery from the stroke, there was no chance that Duke would now accept her into the lung transplant program given her stroke risk.

She ended up fully recovering from her stroke, and was

released from the hospital in a few days. Back on full-time oxygen, and having even more trouble with routine daily tasks, Mom and the full family had no choice but to wait for news from Duke Hospital.

A week later, the dreaded letter arrived.

Dear Judy,

We invite you to be a participant at the Duke Lung Transplant Center Pre-Habilitation program at the Duke Center for Living in Durham, North Carolina.

The letter explained that in this program, if she chose to participate, she would be under the daily supervision of physical therapists trained to help her lose weight and build up strength for a possible lung transplant in the future. There was no guarantee that she would be ever admitted to the program and added to the waiting list. To be part of this exclusive program, she would need to immediately relocate to Durham. Also, she was required to have full-time, live-in family caregiver support. My brother had a job. My sister-in-law had a job. There were no other family members from which to choose, and I was the only one with the flexibility to be able to take on this role.

As Mom read the letter to me, it was clear what needed to be done. "Mom, I'll go there with you," I said.

Leaving my newly formed life in Michigan again was sad. Patrick completely understood what needed to be done, and was supportive. Others in the office understood my predicament and each wished me good luck. I didn't tell any of my clients what was about to happen. Mark drove Mom, in her car, the 12 hours back to Durham. Her breathing had continued to deteriorate over the past several weeks. Mark and Mom located and rented, on a month-to-month contract, a small, dark, dingy two-bedroom apartment near Duke Hospital. I drove from Detroit to Durham in my truck, with my clothes and office stuff, and discretely moved my part of the business to my new bedroom.

After two more days of tests at Duke Hospital, Mom was enrolled in the grueling six-week transplant pre-rehab program at the world-class Center for Living. Every weekday morning, I took Mom to the fitness center and returned in the late afternoon to pick her up. In addition to stretches, floor exercises and light weights, the physical therapists at the center would set Mom up with two tanks of oxygen in a push cart, with a mask like the ones used in the movie *Top Gun* strapped to her face, and instructions to walk as many laps around the indoor track that she could. I was amazed at her strength and fortitude to tackle this physical challenge in spite of her failing lungs. Her daily exercise regimen and a diet of under 1000 calories resulted in, over a few weeks, steady weight loss and an increase in muscle strength.

In the meantime, I did what I could to keep my recruiting business going. Doing most of my work via telephone and computer, I told very few clients that I had left the Detroit area. I could see the momentum that we had built up after the Hill's Angels Action Board intervention starting to wane, and I was unable to travel to meet with potential clients to win new projects. In spite of her impressive weight loss and improvement in muscle strength, Mom's lung function was deteriorating more rapidly. It felt at times as if I were silently observing both the death of my mother and the death of my business. In the meantime, I was paying monthly alimony to Carol with whom I had no contact, and I was paying the mortgage on the empty house in Michigan.

Divorced. Bald. Broke. With no social life. Forty-nine years old and living with my mother in a dark, smelly apartment in a strange city. Not the life of my dreams, but the life in which I find myself. Still setting goals, still striving for balance, still reading and doing what I can to keep myself physically and emotionally healthy, I keep striving for a better day.

Chapter Seven: Believe the Unbelievable

Early in our coaching relationship, Tom advised me to read the book *Synchronicity—The Inner Path of Leadership* by Joseph Jaworski. He said that this book convinced him that there was more out there in the world than we can ever see or understand, and that I would enjoy reading it. Being a good student, I did what he said. I'm sure glad I did.

Flying from Detroit to San Antonio, Texas, for my first SRA conference in 2007, I started reading the book. I wasn't much of a reader at this point in time, so I slugged through it. The book was riveting, and spoke to me in ways I hadn't anticipated. As I read, I looked out the window at the sky and horizon, and pondered what I was learning. The book, written by a scientist and the son of Watergate prosecutor Leon Jaworski, spelled out the proof, partially through his own life experiences, of synchronicity, otherwise called "predictable miracles," in our daily lives.

I've since become convinced that "random occurrences," almost always involving other people, can happen more often if one is aware, open, and prepared or anticipating the event happening. Meeting just the right person, at just the right time, in just the right situation, can be life-changing. It has happened to me over and over, and I'm sure that it has happened to you. On the other hand, if we are too busy, preoccupied, focused on our own stuff and not aware of what's going on around us, we can altogether miss these opportunities, these chance encounters.

I've also learned to be open to inspiration that comes from unexplainable events or through our dreams. Our subconscious brain is at work all the time and creative solutions to our life's challenges can hit when we are least expecting them.

Over the years, Tom has shared with me several fascinating stories of unexplainable things that have happened to him and have changed the course of his life.

One afternoon, when Tom was driving his Harley 54 motorcycle on a rural Missouri country road, he made a familiar sharp turn and headed for the one-lane bridge over Hinkson Creek. He had been over this bridge a hundred times before, and there was never, ever any traffic on this road. On this particular day, as he made the turn, he was greeted by a big commercial plumbing truck, coming right for him, and taking up the entire road. Tom had two choices; one— drive off the road and into the ditch, most definitely getting killed or severely injured as a result. The other option—close his eyes and keep on driving. He closed his eyes. When he opened his eyes, he was driving on the other side of the truck, untouched. Unbelievable? Absolutely. Unexplainable? Of course. True? It happened. Tom's only explanation—it was not his time to go.

> **True but unexplainable.**

Tom Hill is not a make believe kind of guy. He'll be the first to tell you that he is left-brained, very logical, always on time, and not very creative. He is skeptical of things that can't be proved with data and with science. He's not gullible, simply believes in the facts. It is his nature as a person that makes this motorcycle story all the more fascinating. True but unexplainable.

In 1973, after divorcing Carol and venturing out in life as a single, lonely father of four, whose kids lived two hundred miles away, Tom had bouts of desperate sadness. One Sunday morning, with nothing else to do to occupy his time, he decided to clean the small trailer in which he was living. He turned on his portable radio. Usually listening to FM stations, the switch was somehow set on AM. Scanning through the various rural stations available, he came across a program. The voice on the other end introduced himself as a member of the Kendrick United Methodist Church in Jackson, Missouri—10 miles from where Tom was living. The speaker was not a preacher, but just a regular guy who shared his testimony. Tom was overcome with emotion, got down on his hands and knees, cried, prayed, read from the Bible, and at the end of the message, which lasted about an hour, Tom wrote the name of the speaker and the church. Tom said to himself, "I've got to go meet this guy."

Tom got dressed and drove over to Jackson, found the small church, and saw that people were arriving for the weekly service. Tom found the pastor greeting folks at the front door, and told him that he had heard the great radio program earlier that morning. Tom shared the name of the speaker and asked if he could thank him. With a perplexed look on his face, the pastor responded, "Sir, our church does not have a radio program—never had and probably never will. Jackson's a very small town. Also, we don't have anyone here by that name." Tom argued for a bit, trying to convince the pastor that they do indeed have a radio program, and that he had listened to the service that morning.

As the pastor slowly closed the front door, Tom stood there dumbfounded and a bit in shock. Now convinced that the lay preacher did not in fact exist, Tom walked away with a new peace and knowing; confident that everything will somehow be okay.

What happened really happened. True but unexplainable.

In 1991, life was good! Tom and Betty were living in their beautiful home in Nashville, Tennessee, and business was fantastic. Two of Tom's daughters and a son-in-law were all working for the company. Healthy and financially secure, Tom and Betty were living the life of their dreams.

Pause. Tom soon had a dream, literally.

In this dream, it was clear as day that he and Betty would sell their ownership in RE/MAX of Kentucky, Tennessee, and the Southern Ohio regions, and they would purchase the full ownership rights to RE/MAX of Mississippi, Alabama, and Louisiana. In this dream, they would sell their house in Nashville, and move to Jackson, Mississippi. They would fire their three kids who worked for them. Logically, this dream made no sense. They loved living in Nashville. They loved having their kids around. There was no way that Howard, his business partner, would support this crazy scheme. Tom's dream had truth and wisdom in it. Betty was completely supportive, and said, "Tom, let's go for it!" When he shared with Howard the idea, Howard quickly agreed and said that it was a great idea. The kids took the change well. The move to Mississippi went quickly and smoothly, and the business took off like a rocket. This business move, triggered by a crazy dream, ended up being the tipping point in the evolution of Tom's entrepreneurial journey.

In 2012 Tom had another dream. He dreamed that he would somehow touch one million lives. About this time, he met Gary Baker, who subsequently became the brainchild and driver of the Tom Hill Institute, Arête, and the Emerging

Leaders Organization—all aimed at helping people and all part of the platform that is enabling Tom's dream of touching one million lives.

You, by reading this book, are part of that one million.

Chapter Eight: One Person, Attracted to You

I've heard him say it a hundred times. That must mean he's said it a million times, and therefore he must surely believe it. I know he does, and he has tons of examples to share from his own life, and from the lives of other people.

> *"One person, attracted to you because of who you have become, can change your life forever."*

When I first heard this from Tom, I thought he was talking about that **one** single person, the **one** who most significantly changed, or will in the future change, your life forever. I've since come to learn that it's not about one single other person, but more about the one **you**, and the one **me**, and the actions that we take to become the very best people we can. From that foundation, we will attract into our lives several, perhaps dozens or even hundreds, of other people who will change our lives forever.

The key is becoming the very best individuals that we can. And this doesn't stop. This doesn't stop after high school, after college, after getting married or having kids, after landing that great job, or even after retirement. This process of being the very best person that we can goes on for a lifetime. People that get this, that commit to it, are the ones who seem to have all the luck, and seem to attract the right people into their lives.

Tom is one of these people, and I am sure trying to become one as well.

After selling his final shares of his RE/MAX business, Tom had time on his hands and was financially secure. People came out of the woodwork to ask him how he did it. How did an egghead professor, with no sales or business experience, go on to so quickly build such a successful real estate business? People regularly asked Tom to speak to their groups and to coach them individually.

As Tom shifted his time and energy into coaching and speaking, he also became an avid student of people and success, curious about why some people "get it," and most others don't. He saw this phenomenon within the one-hundred franchisees of his RE/MAX business, and began to articulate his principles of success, as well as created a structure—a curriculum for his coaching approach.

While previously running his RE/MAX businesses, Tom had started a mastermind group with five other RE/MAX regional owners. The group met once per quarter for three days, over a time period lasting three years. For one of these meetings, Tom invited motivational speaker and author, Mark Victor Hansen, as a guest. Mark, along with Jack Canfield, were co-founders of the incredibly successful *Chicken Soup for the Soul* series of books, of which over 500 million copies have been sold. Mark accepted Tom's invitation, and attended day three of one of these unique meetings. Mark and Tom became friends and stayed in touch over the years to follow.

During this same time period, and after selling his RE/MAX interests, Tom remained a big follower of his hero, Jim Rohn, and attended several Jim Rohn seminars. As a result of this, Tom became friends with the owner of Jim Rohn International,

Kyle Wilson. Kyle Wilson later collaborated with Hansen and Canfield to write a new Chicken Soup book to be titled, *Chicken Soup for the Entrepreneur's Soul*. As part of this book project, Kyle asked Tom Hill if he would be a coauthor on the new book. Tom's obvious and immediate answer—"yes!"

Tom already had an idea brewing in his head for a different book, and decided to take a three-day solitude trip to write the draft. Tom recommends to each of his coaching clients that they take a three-day solitude trip, without human interaction, at least twice per year. During Tom's alone-time in a cabin in the woods, while listening to baroque music recorded at sixty beats per minute, Tom sat down and wrote the full draft of his first novel, *Living at the Summit*. Tom has found that listening to this type of music is a great way to improve creativity and concentration.

As Tom and Kyle Wilson developed *Chicken Soup for the Entrepreneur's Soul*, Tom became friends with attorney John Gardner and his wife, Elizabeth. John and Elizabeth proved to be very helpful in the editing and publishing of *Living at the Summit*, and Tom decided it would be great if John could also be a coauthor on the new Chicken Soup book. After calling Jack Canfield to request permission to add John Gardner as a coauthor, Jack responded that this was very unlikely, given there was already another coauthor.

Eighteen months later, as Tom and Betty delivered the first 5000 copies of *Living at the Summit* to the Gardners, living at that time in Nashville, Tom received a phone call from Jack Canfield. Jack shared that he wanted to go ahead and let John and Elizabeth Gardner be coauthors of *Chicken Soup for the Entrepreneur's Soul*. Needless to say, Tom, Betty, John and Elizabeth were all giddy with excitement.

From setting up a mastermind group to bravely inviting

Mark Victor Hansen. From meeting Kyle Wilson to becoming friends with John and Elizabeth Gardner. From a phone call to Jack Canfield and being initially being denied. This story clearly reflects the principle of **"One Person, Attracted to You Because of Who You Have Become, Can Change Your Life Forever."** Coauthoring *Chicken Soup for the Entrepreneur's Soul* changed Tom Hill's life forever, and would not have been possible if not for the supporting cast of folks he attracted into his life because of who he had become.

The "one person attracted to you because of who you have become," can be that one super-special person, your spouse. After three years of living on his own, and climbing the ladder within the academic world, Tom was not interested in meeting any new lady friends. Focused on being a good father to his four fast growing kids, as well as his own personal and professional growth, being in a new romantic relationship was not a priority. But Terri and Terri had other ideas.

Terri Hill, Tom's second-oldest child, and her new classmate at Southeast Missouri State University, Terri Camp, had become close friends. Soon realizing that both of their parents were divorced, and after Terri Hill met Terri Camp's beautiful mother, they discretely set about lining up a blind date. How cool would it be if we were real sisters, they thought. Starting with Terri Camp's mom, Betty Camp, they encouraged her to be open to meeting Terri Hill's father, Tom Hill. At this time, Betty was divorced and the secretary for a CEO at a large a manufacturing company in St. Louis. She was very self-sufficient, and not in a hurry to meet a new guy. Tom, who was living in Cape Girardeau, Missouri, a two hour drive from St. Louis where Betty lived, was the regional director for the University of Missouri Extension Service. After repeated prodding from daughter Terri, Tom finally gave into the pressure to go on a date with Betty. Their first date, July 1, 1979, was to a St. Louis Cardinals baseball game. In October 1979, Tom proposed, and on May 10, 1980, Tom and Betty were married. 35 years later, their marriage remains a storybook romance, with a mutual love and respect that has grown over the years. Tom is convinced that without his several years of personal growth, he would not have attracted Betty into his life. Tom is now, as he is famous for quoting,

"Blessed beyond measure."

* * *

Living in this apartment is starting to get old. I'm somehow keeping the business afloat, and Mom and I haven't killed each other yet in sharing this cramped space. I love her, but spending this much time together is starting to take its toll on the both of us. Mom is steadily losing weight and getting stronger from the daily visits to the Center for Living, and I've been able to find time during the day, and even sometimes at night, to get out of the apartment. I've taken some long runs on the trails in the nearby beautiful Duke Forest, and on the treadmill at night at the Center for Living.

Not knowing how many weeks or months this process may take, I was getting restless. There was no guarantee that the doctors at Duke Hospital would accept Mom as a potential transplant recipient, and if she were allowed to go on the waiting list, the wait time was impossible to predict. I had met several patients who had been waiting for over six months, some even over a year. As a patient on the transplant waiting list, you were required to live within a 30-minute drive from the hospital, and have family caregiver support on-call at all times, 24/7. I pictured myself living here in Durham for quite a long time.

I'm a recruiter. I'm a guy. I'm lonely. This will be simple, I'll use technology. Firing up my laptop, I logged into my old eHarmony account—the one I had stopped using in Michigan. Not expecting to meet anyone for the long run, especially since I was only going to be in Durham until my mom either had her surgery or something worse took place, I thought it would be okay if I just met some ladies to hang out with. Updating my eHarmony profile, I put even more emphasis on health and spirituality. I knew that any girl I met needed to be healthy, preferably a runner, be optimistic and a Christian. After changing the physical location of my profile from Brighton, Michigan, to Durham, North Carolina, I pressed "OK" to initiate the process. I was curious to see the results. With eHarmony, unlike other dating sites, you are notified the following day, or later, of any matches to your profile.

Back to business as usual, I tried to focus on work, my life, and helping my mom. Still being coached by Tom Hill on a monthly basis, I continued to read, to grow, to eat healthy foods and get plenty of exercise. I took Mom to the downtown Durham Methodist Church on Sunday mornings, which was becoming increasingly difficult as her breathing steadily deteriorated. I found the super-traditional nature of this old church to be not what I was looking for, but I still felt the presence of God during the services. I knew it meant the world to Mom to be able to go to church.

Three weeks after launching my new eHarmony campaign, I had a number of ladies in the queue that looked interesting. Having talked with two on the telephone, I arranged a date with one who looked like she had potential. A date for dinner was scheduled for the following week. Two days later, a new profile was sent my way via the folks at eHarmony. Her name was Kim. I was mesmerized by her photo, and liked what I read about her profile. Following the normal eHarmony process, Kim and I went back and forth with the guided questions politely getting to know each other. As soon as I was allowed by the system, I sent an email to Kim asking if it would be okay if I called her. She responded with a "yes," and gave me her number, suggesting a time I could call.

The following afternoon I called Kim at 5:30, she answered, and the attraction started immediately. While on that first call, I asked Kim if I could friend her on Facebook. She said, "Yes," thinking that I would do this later. She was surprised when the Facebook friend request hit her cell phone immediately. Kim and I then enjoyed getting to know each other, our families and some of our history through Facebook posts and photos. I was amazed at what I learned about this special lady, and loved every minute of talking with her. A little skeptical of what was yet to be found, I recognized that I was feeling both chemistry and compatibility with this beautiful girl. Kim and I talked every night, for a couple of hours, for three straight days. Knowing I already had a date for the coming Thursday night, and that I would be out of town for the weekend (I was going back to Michigan to run the Brighton Half Marathon), we scheduled a date for the following Sunday, immediately after my return to Durham.

I met my previously scheduled date at a Japanese restaurant in Cary. She was a nice person, but my mind was on Kim the entire evening. As soon as dinner was over, I asked for the check, paid for dinner and politely, I hope, escorted my friend to her car. Giving her a quick hug goodbye, I immediately returned to my car, where I picked up my cell phone and called Kim. It was 9:30 p.m. Kim answered with a giggle in her voice.

I said hello and asked her if I was interrupting anything. She said, "No," that she had just walked into her apartment after dinner and drinks with some girlfriends. She asked what I was doing, and I said I just finished dinner at a Japanese restaurant. "Awww," she said, "were you out all by yourself?" I could tell she was genuinely concerned for me. "Umm, no, I was on a date."

"Can I come over?" I couldn't believe I had just said that. This would be breaking all the dating rules and it would be the first time we ever met.

"Sure," she replied.

Using the GPS on my cell phone for navigation, I was bummed as my cell battery died just before entering her sprawling apartment complex. It was pitch dark outside, and I was lost. As I drove down the main drive, I noticed what appeared to be cute lady walking barefoot in the parking lot. I slowed and pulled close to her, lowering my window. "Brett?" she said. By this time, under a street light, I recognized that this was the same beautiful lady that I had been talking with and corresponding with on Facebook and eHarmony for the past few days. "Hi, Kim, it's me."

She came around to the passenger door, opened and sat down, and gave me a hug. "Do you want to come in?"

As we went into her small but well decorated apartment, Kim poured a couple of glasses of wine, and we sat down on the couch. Just like something out of true love in high school, the energy and attraction was immediate and intense, and we spent hours that evening talking and getting to know each other. Driving home to the apartment I shared with my mother later that evening, I was amazed at how compatible Kim and I appeared to be, and I couldn't shake off the intense attraction I felt. The date —July 1, 2010, was 31 years to the day of when Tom Hill and Betty Camp had their first date on July 1, 1979, the year I graduated from high school. In 1979, Kim was ten years old. As Tom Hill is so fond of saying,

"You just can't make this stuff up."

Kim had been single for several years, having sadly lost her husband to suicide. She shared that history with me on our first phone call. I shared that I was divorced and that I learned a lot about my previous codependency. Kim was also codependent in her marriage. Our common language of personal growth, striving for independence, health, spirituality, love of family, and optimism for the future further attracted us to each other.

Kim had been using eHarmony for several months, having moved to Durham the previous year from Jacksonville, Florida. Her previous eHarmony dates were just average, and she had some very funny stories of her dating encounters. Kim shared that after initially ruling out men very quickly, a friend advised her to give guys another chance. So, she identified three deal-breaker rules:

- They could not be married
- They could not be gay, or could not be more feminine than her
- They could not live with their mother

I obviously failed rule number three, and I fully disclosed the nature of my living situation during our first phone call. Instead of being disqualified for failing this rule, I received extra credit for being a caregiver, and showing so much love to my mom. Lucky me!

Kim and Mom met a couple of times, but it was getting

increasingly more difficult for Mom to get out of the apartment, other than for the required trips to the Center for Living and tests at Duke Hospital. Kim, who had a great job at Blue Cross and Blue Shield of North Carolina, came by several times after work to visit me and to check on Mom.

On Sunday mornings, I would take Mom to the early service at Durham United Methodist Church, take her home, and then meet Kim at her church, newhope church (yes, it's intentionally all lowercased) in Durham. I loved this church, and also loved attending with Kim. This whole new relationship was feeling too good to be true.

On July 28, 2010, we received great news. Mom got a call from Duke Hospital telling her that she would now be officially placed on the lung transplant waiting list. This was an answer to our prayers, and we were all so happy! Having now been with Mom nearly daily for the past two months, I was ready for a break. I called my brother Mark and shared the good news with him, and asked if he wouldn't mind staying with Mom for the weekend while Kim and I went on a short trip to the mountains. Mark agreed, and flew up to Raleigh-Durham a few days later. While packing for our trip the next morning, Mark called. "What are you doing?" he said.

"Packing for our trip," I replied.

"You should hold off."

"Why?"

"Doctor called—got lungs. I'm taking Mom to the hospital now," he shared.

I couldn't believe what I was hearing. She was on the waiting list less than two days. Now, she's getting a transplant? I called Kim at work and told her what I had just heard, and she said she'd meet us at the hospital. Two hours later, Mom was in the operating room waiting for her new set of lungs to arrive, while Mark, Kim and I hung out in the waiting room. A nice way for Mark and Kim to get to know each other. Eight hours later, we learned that Mom's surgery was complete and was successful, and the next day we were allowed to go back to her recovery room to see her. With a breathing tube in her mouth, and lines, wires, and drainage tubes coming out from all around her body, Mom was alive and breathing. As she groggily opened her eyes, she saw the three of us looking down upon her. Thus began a new life with a new pair of lungs from an anonymous donor, but also a new life with the daily threat of lung rejection.

Mom recovered well from her transplant surgery, which included daily workouts back at the Center for Living. On September 30, Mark flew to Durham and then accompanied Mom on a flight back to her home in Florida. Kim and I drove Mom's car, along with her clothes and other belongings, back to her home in Niceville. We were all together, with tears of joy, to celebrate the miracle of Mom's new lungs as she walked on the beautiful white sand beach at Destin, freely breathing the fresh air that we all otherwise take for granted.

Kim and I had a decision to make. We were falling in love with each other. My mom was now home in Florida, and I had a home and a business in Michigan. Our options:

- We break up and I move back to Michigan alone
- Kim quits her job at Blue Cross, and moves to Michigan with me
- I stay in North Carolina, and run my business remotely

I had noticed that the business was starting to pick up a bit, and when I traveled to Michigan, I was able to win business fairly quickly. We decided to give the third option a try, with me staying at her condominium. I rented office space from one of Kim's girlfriends, which gave me a place to work during the day.

As Mom got stronger, the relationship with Kim and I grew as well. Free now to travel as much as necessary, I made frequent trips to Michigan to focus on the recruiting business. I enjoyed getting to know Kim's sister, Sharon, her husband and two kids living in nearby Cary. I also met many of Kim's friends and co-workers at Blue Cross.

Kim and I trained together, and then ran the City of Oaks Half Marathon in Raleigh on November 7, 2010. I pinched myself that I was actually dating a girl who could run a half marathon. I had been misled on this point so many times before, and knew how important a real commitment to physical health was to me. Kim and I visited her parents over Thanksgiving at their home in Aiken, South Carolina, and I loved getting to know both of them.

Kim surprised me by offering to take me to Italy for my 50th birthday, which was on March 13, 2011. We set up a joint savings account, and saved all of the money in advance. What a wonderful idea, and we had an amazing, romantic time.

All three of my kids soon met Kim, and they loved her. We took a trip to Missouri to visit my dad and his wife, Pam, and they loved her as well.

As part of my coaching relationship with Tom Hill, he insisted that before I got seriously involved in a romantic relationship, he and Betty needed to meet and approve my choice. I knew this was half a joke, but I was also eager to have Kim, Tom and Betty get to know each other. Kim and I signed up for the world-famous "Indy-Mini," which is the largest half marathon in the world, with over 30,000 runners. Tom and his son-in-law, Eric were also scheduled to run this half marathon, which was held in Indianapolis, Indiana.

Nina, Betty's daughter, and Eric lived in nearby Carmel, Indiana, and we were invited to their house for dinner the evening before the big race. As Kim and I were greeted at the front door, I noticed that all the attention was on Kim, getting to know her and to see if she might be the "one" for Brett. Kim was absolutely herself throughout the entire evening, and was completely loved by all those folks who already loved me. The next day Tom discreetly shared with me how much he, Betty and Nina liked Kim, and he gave me Betty's official approval to proceed.

Kim and I attended my nephew Ryan's wedding to his wife Bailey in Destin, Florida, in June, and also took part in Kim's family vacation in Myrtle Beach, South Carolina, in July.

On November 6, 2011, Kim and I ran our third half marathon together, this one being again the Raleigh City of Oaks.

As our relationship continued to grow and solidify, I knew that this was the girl I wanted to spend the rest of my life with. We had now rented a house together, and compatibility was not a question. Chemistry was also a given, as we were magnetically drawn together whenever we had a chance.

On November 20th, I proposed to Kim at P.F. Chang's restaurant in Durham, during a date with my mom there as well. Mom was in town for tests at Duke Hospital, and we had also arranged an early Thanksgiving celebration as an opportunity for Mom to meet Kim's sister, family, and her parents who were in town. Mom knew ahead of time what I had planned, and I had previously shown her the engagement ring that I had purchased. Setting it up so that Mom would excuse herself to go to the restroom, I got down on one knee and proposed. As I pretended to be tying my shoe, Kim jokingly said, "What are you doing down there, proposing?"

"Well, actually, I am," I responded as I showed her the ring hiding in the palm of my hand.

"Will you marry me?"

"Oh my God, yes!" she exclaimed, and we kissed and hugged as Mom came back to the table.

We couldn't wait to tell people at church, for by this time we were both active volunteers and had built quite a circle of friends there. Our plan was to go to the early service that coming Sunday, and then talk to Pastor Benji afterward to ask if he would marry us. As we visited with people in the church rotunda prior to the service, I was beaming with pride, and couldn't resist showing as many people as I knew Kim's ring, which I had proudly designed.

Settling into seats much closer to the front than we typically use, the service began. Music, lights, cool graphics… the worship service is very uplifting and energized, yet at the same time always opens my heart for hearing the message. I was especially alive that morning, holding the hand of my new fiancée.

Pastor Benji's message that morning was on dating and marriage. Great, I thought, and I was proud that I had been lucky enough to fall in love with a lady who had the same faith and priorities about faith and the church in her life. It all felt perfect, until Pastor Benji went on a rant about the sin of folks shacking up prior to marriage. I had been living with Kim for over one year. We rationalized this in all kinds of different ways, but bottom line, we were living together. Pastor Benji, with grace but truth, made it clear that he didn't agree with unmarried people living together, although it goes on all the time, and if he was aware that a couple was indeed "shacking up" prior to marriage, then he would not conduct the marriage ceremony.

Kim and I quietly left the service after it was over, like puppies with their tails between their legs. As we made the short drive home, in silence, we both pondered what to do next.

Four weeks later, on December 30, 2011, we eloped in Asheville, North Carolina. No one knew about the ceremony in advance other than the funky lady reverend we found online, the photographer and the two guys who ran the bed and breakfast where we stayed and where we held our private ceremony. It was a beautiful event, and we will forever have fond memories of Asheville and the surrounding area.

In May of 2012, Kim and I rented a house at Santa Rosa Beach near Destin, Florida, and had a big party with family and friends to celebrate our marriage. We had a wonderful time.

A year later, Kim and I bought a beautiful home in southwest Durham, with a very short commute to her office at Blue Cross, and with a great office space upstairs from which I can work at home. The neighborhood has a two-mile running trail, as well as a clubhouse with a fitness center and pool. It's less than two miles from our beloved church as well as the American Tobacco Trail, where we love to train on our longer runs. We pinch ourselves every day for the blessing of this home.

For the past four years, Kim and I have grown deeply in love, sharing a common language of independence and commitment to personal growth. With our Christian faith as a cornerstone, we have an amazing relationship. Following what I have learned from Tom Hill, I know that I attracted Kim to me because of the person I had become, and because of the person that I am committed to being. Kim attracted me into her life for the same reasons.

We both feel absolutely blessed beyond measure, and we somehow both know that the best in our marriage is yet to come, as we continue to grow as individuals and as a couple.

"One person, attracted to you, because of who you have become..." those words ring strong in my head. They are a regular reminder to stay focused on my own personal growth, to be clear of my priorities, to stay open to synchronicity, to stay disciplined and resilient, patient and hopeful for great things to come. Knowing that this steady approach to my life is the best way to put the odds in my favor, I can also reflect upon many other people whom I have attracted into my life as I have been on my growth path.

In addition to Kim, some of these people are:

<u>Tom Hill:</u> When I was 22 years young, Tom saw something in me that I didn't see in myself. In spite of the relationship ending with his daughter, Michelle, Tom and I were later to reconnect in the beginnings of the RE/MAX days—setting the stage for a life-long relationship that would be instrumental in setting the trajectory of the second half of my adult life.

<u>Al Curtis and Sandi Maki</u>: When I first met Al and Sandi at that Toastmasters meeting in Brighton, Michigan, I knew that there was something special about these two. In addition to opening my eyes to the incredible power of social media and innovative marketing techniques, they also brought me under their wings and helped me reorient my thinking about money, risk, and commitment as an entrepreneur. Forever my soul mates, I will always be thankful for both Al and Sandi for the impact they have had on my life.

<u>Gary Soloway</u>: Gary and I put together my first mastermind group while I was living in my apartment in Murfreesboro, Tennessee. Being a great friend during an especially difficult

time in my life, Gary gave me hope and perspective for what my life would be like post-divorce. Also an excellent businessman and wise counsel, Gary and his wife Tricia have become dear friends.

Roger Hall: As with many of my friends and influencers over the past half-dozen years, I met Dr. Roger Hall at an Eagle Summit. Becoming fast friends, I eventually signed up as a student in his High Performance Advisory (HPA) Academy, where he taught me the academic and practical foundation for being a qualified life coach. I am forever thankful to Roger for sharing his professional experience, enthusiasm, and genuine concern for my wellbeing and future. I am proud to be a graduate of Dr. Hall's HPA program, and honored to be his friend.

Gary Baker: Another great individual whom I met at an Eagle Summit, I am forever blessed to have crossed Gary's path. Inspired by Gary's relentless creativity in forming new business ideas, I am thankful to be a part of the Arête and Emerging Leader Organization. Gary has been instrumental in advising me through the formation of my coaching and consulting business, Blair Leadership Group, and he has taught me, through his own successful example, the power of setting a vision for my business and then bringing that vision to reality.

Courtney Grant Tobbe: As the most tenured employee in the SRA firm, Courtney has been working with me since early 2008. Having been through all of the trials and tribulations that the company has endured, along with my roller-coaster existence as the owner and president, Courtney has been the rock that has held everything together. Taking care of details related to the operating of the office, and someone I trust like family, I am free to invest my time and energy into working *on* the business, and *on* myself, as opposed to working *in* the business. Courtney is a trusted colleague and dear friend.

<u>Brian Hagman</u>: Early in my recruiting business, Brian Hagman was a client. As the human resources manager of one of the companies that my firm was recruiting for, Brian and I became friends over the years. Recognizing that Brian was an entrepreneur-in-waiting, we discussed ways that he could leave his corporate job, and take the leap to working in my firm. In January 2012, Brian did the courageous thing and launched his life of self-employment. A key business partner, Brian has grown significantly in his contribution to the company, and is on the path to great success in the future.

<u>Curt Steinhorst</u>: After his presentation at an Eagle Summit, I approached Curt to learn more about his business. We hit it off immediately. Curt, as a professional speaker and speech coach, helped me immensely in crafting and delivering several live presentations. During the process of working closely with Curt as my speech coach, we have developed a close friendship. I thank Curt for the excellent support he has provided to me as I have grown as a speaker and communicator.

<u>Alice Osborn</u>: This book would not have been possible without the assistance of Alice Osborn. As an expert author, editor, and writing coach, Alice has been instrumental in getting this project organized and off the ground. This is the third book that I've attempted, with the previous books being tossed aside after a futile effort. Alice taught me the incredible power of using the Hero's Journey as a literary process, and she has been a constant source of encouragement and counsel as the various phases of this book were developed.

I could go on and on, but I'll stop with this list. My point is this—none of these people would be in my life if I had not attracted them to me because of the person I have become, and because of the person I am becoming.

In addition to the right people being attracted to you because of who you have become, the same principles apply with finances. Money is not pursued, but is attracted to you by the value that you provide to the marketplace. As an individual becomes more and more healthy, balanced, and proficient in their field, they also become more valuable in the marketplace. This value, over time, will reveal itself, and one's worth in terms of money will simply increase.

> *Money is not pursued, but is attracted to you by the value that you provide to the marketplace.*

Tom always says,

> *"You should work harder on yourself than you do on your job."*

By doing this you will become increasingly more and more capable, generous, healthy, loving, aware, insightful … the list can go on and on. Who doesn't want to put the odds greatly in their favor for personal and financial success?

I'm committed to this life-long process of ongoing personal growth by focusing on my six priority areas of life, and I can't wait to see what unfolds ahead for me as a result.

Chapter Nine: One Idea, Well Executed

It was a hot, humid afternoon in the summer of 1984. The air conditioning in his office in the old building where he worked at the University of Missouri could barely keep up with the escalating temperatures and humidity outside. Tom just wrapped up another one of the seemingly endless conference calls with several of his staff members in the field. Tom was the Director of the State 4-H program, with over 100,000 4-H'ers involved, 20,000 volunteers, and a staff of 130. Busy? No doubt. An important job? Sure, they did good work for the state. Inspiring? Not a good answer to that one.

"Hey, when you have a second, you should listen to these," Bob said as he tossed a couple of cassette tapes on Tom's desk. "What is this?" Tom replied. "Some guy I listened to at the seminar I went to last weekend. His name is Jim Rohn. I think you'll like him." Bob was a staffer in Tom Hill's 4-H organization, and he knew that Tom was a little restless in his career at the university. "Who the heck is Jim Rohn?" Tom thought to himself.

Tom listened to the tapes, and his mind started racing. He quickly grasped that Jim Rohn was a business philosopher, not a motivational speaker. Tom and Betty then listened to the tapes together, several times until they wore out. As the ancient saying goes, "When the student is ready, the teacher will appear." For Tom, Jim Rohn was that teacher, and Tom was ready to listen and be his student. One of the things that Jim Rohn said on the recording was,

"How tall should a tree grow?"
The answer, "As tall as it can."

After listening to this, Betty paused the cassette player, turned to Tom and said, "Honey, you haven't grown as tall as you can." She said this with love, respect and admiration for her husband, and as a genuine supporter and encourager in his life.

Betty believed in Tom well before he believed in himself.

Tom and Betty then began a process of contemplation and ongoing discussion of what was important for their lives, for their marriage and family, and for their legacy. They both began to realize that the comfortable, yet bureaucratic and limiting life as a university professor may not be the calling for them. Tom continued to do his job, to perform very well at the university, and to be a great husband and father. He was also searching, pondering, considering his future, and becoming increasingly uncomfortable and ready to make a change. Tom and Betty discussed what was important for each of them, and they ranked their priorities, as a couple, on the six areas of life.

Taking a six-month leave of absence from his position at the University of Missouri, Tom and Betty's first attempt at entrepreneurship didn't fly. Starting a small seminar company, they soon found that their typical audience, usually first-line supervisors, was not quite suited for the content being taught. In this new venture they did not make a dime, but this failure did not deter them from their determination for a better future. Tom eventually returned to his role at the university, buying time until the right opportunity presented itself.

In January 1986 Tom and Betty went on vacation to Florida. To break up the drive, they visited one of Tom's college roommates who now lived in Atlanta. His name was Howard, and at this time Howard owned the rights to RE/MAX Real Estate of Georgia. Howard was seeing great success with RE/MAX, which was a new concept in the real estate industry, and was growing like crazy all across the country. Tom had no idea what RE/MAX was, but was certainly willing to listen. Tom shared with Howard his ongoing frustrations with life at the university, the bureaucracy, and the challenges of getting promoted. During this meeting, Howard suggested that Tom leave the university, and move to Georgia to sell RE/MAX franchises in the regions outside of Atlanta. For anyone who knows Georgia, that doesn't leave a significant number of potential markets. The idea was that if, just if, Tom was successful in selling RE/MAX franchises in Georgia, then he and Howard could potentially become partners in ownership of other RE/MAX regions throughout the country.

As Tom and Betty drove back to Columbia from their vacation, they discussed the idea that Howard had shared. Betty was completely and fully supportive; she suggested to Tom that they "go for it." When they got home, Tom called Howard and said, "Yes, I'm in. Let's get started."

Eighteen months after listening to the Jim Rohn tapes, Tom decided to resign from the University of Missouri. He and Betty cashed in their 26-year retirement savings, paid off their mortgage and other debts, sold one of their two cars and almost all of their belongings, and with $36,000 to their name, embarked upon an unknown career in selling something called a RE/MAX real estate franchise.

At this time, Tom had two kids in college and one in high

school, with plans to go to college. He had zero experience in the real estate profession, and had never sold a thing in his life. On the other hand, Tom had great confidence in the RE/MAX concept, of one-hundred percent commission to agents, who in turn paid a flat fee to their brokers, and he had confidence in his own ability to be able to sell this concept to potential prospects in the market. He knew he was being exposed to a great idea, and if he could execute it well, it could change his life forever. At the time, he didn't know how right he would be.

When Tom told his colleagues, family and friends of his decision to leave the university for a new life as a real estate franchise salesperson, most thought he had completely lost his mind. Not only was he starting in a brand new line of work, he was moving 1000 miles away from his family and friends. The criticism was intense and relentless, but Tom and Betty stayed true to their beliefs in themselves and the opportunity they saw in front of them.

In February 1986, Tom attended a weeklong RE/MAX training program at their headquarters in Denver, Colorado. He left that week super-charged to get started, and asked himself, "Who do I know in the real estate world who could help me in selling franchises?" His answer—no one. Tom simply did not know a soul who had this type of experience. He did, however, have the foresight to know that he would need help to be successful in Georgia in this new venture.

One afternoon while I was at work at 3M, I received a phone call. It was Dr. Hill. By this time, Michelle and I had been broken-up for over a year. I had no idea what Tom would be calling me about. I had been making my car payments, so I didn't think it had to do with the loan. On the call, Tom said that he had some exciting news, and asked to meet me for breakfast at the Burger King. I met Tom the next morning, and he shared with me his excitement about his upcoming entrepreneurial journey. At this point in my life, I was very disillusioned with my job at 3M. I was becoming convinced that engineering was not right for me. I was frustrated that my boss and his superiors in the company would not assign me for one of several projects including travel to Japan even though I spoke the language. I was simply at a crossroads in my career. When Tom shared his excitement, I became excited as well, and we soon discussed and agreed on a plan where I would resign from my job at 3M, and join him in selling RE/MAX franchises. My entrepreneurial mind, which had been quieted since my early teen years, was starting to fire back up.

When I resigned from 3M, my family and friends thought I was crazy. I started to see a pattern of this, as these same people thought I was crazy when I chose to spend a year in Tokyo. Little by little, I found myself being comfortable going against the grain of "normal" in some of the decisions I was making. I sold my condominium, sold most of my furniture, and loaded up my Pontiac Fiero for the one thousand mile trek to Savannah, Georgia.

Just as Tom had no experience in selling, neither had I. I read up as much as I could, and I challenged myself to be brave and courageous in handling the sales process and the relentless rejection that comes from cold calling. Tom was a great boss and mentor, and we had some wonderful times in the first several months of selling, or for me, attempting to sell, RE/MAX franchises in rural Georgia. I was 25 years old, a degreed industrial engineer, a little shy and with no sales experience. I was attempting to sell a $15,000 "idea" to real estate brokers scattered throughout South Georgia, most of whom were at least twice my age. In spite of my earnest efforts, I was not very successful, but I did learn a lot. I learned about myself, about dealing with people, about planning and self-motivation. I faced fear and made the calls anyway. I was rejected and rejected and rejected again, but kept on "keeping on."

Over the next seven years, Tom would go on to prove to be extremely successful as a RE/MAX franchise salesperson and as the owner of several RE/MAX regions. Tom's maturity (notice I didn't say "age" out of respect for the old guy), his ability to tailor his sales approach to the right brain versus left brain attributes of his prospects, and his persistence and tough-minded determination to get the job done, all worked together to lead to his success.

After acquiring the rights to RE/MAX of Kentucky, Tom and Howard were then offered and purchased the rights to RE/MAX of Southern Ohio. Tom continued to sell franchises at a very fast pace, and was soon the most successful RE/MAX salesperson in the country of all time. This success led to the opportunity to purchase RE/MAX of Mississippi/Alabama/Louisiana, again in partnership with Howard. During the first eight months, Tom and Betty would move from Tybee Island, Georgia to Atlanta then to Nashville, Tennessee. They absolutely loved Nashville, but to continue to grow the business, after acquiring the full ownership of the Mississippi/Alabama/Louisiana region in 1990, they moved to Brandon, Mississippi, near Jackson. This proved to be a great decision for Tom, and he ultimately owned a RE/MAX region made up of three states, with over three billion dollars in sales and one thousand agents. In 1993, Tom sold 25 percent of the business to a new partner, who would also take over the day-to-day operations. Tom and Betty found themselves with "time and money," and in 1994, to be closer to family, they moved home to St. Louis. In 1999, Tom sold his remaining 75 percent of the

RE/MAX business to his partner, Howard, and at that point was fully disconnected from the business.

From the Jim Rohn tapes being tossed on his desk in the summer of 1984, to becoming the most successful RE/MAX sales person in 1986, Tom proved that significant life change can occur, and at any age. Tom went on to be extremely successful as the owner of his fast-growing business, and grew tremendously in his professional capabilities and in his financial well-being. As Tom's fast and dramatic success in the RE/MAX world became well known, he found people coming to him, from all across the country, asking, "Tom, how in the world did you do that? How did you go from being a middle-aged college professor to a successful entrepreneur? Would you help me?" Of course, Tom wanted to help these folks.

Tom was also fascinated by his observations of how some RE/MAX owners, either of full-regions or of individual real estate offices, would be hugely successful, and why others would fail, either quickly or eventually. He expanded this observation across other parts of his life, and started to develop a passion around understanding personal growth and success. Why, within the same family and with the same parents and environment, will one sibling be very successful in life while another struggles? Why are some people healthy and vibrant while others make no effort to improve their health, instead choosing to accept chronic illness, weakness and pain? Why do some people have a passion for learning, reading and intellectual growth, while many are content watching television? Why do some people trade their time for money, in jobs they hate, while others are creating value through their passions and entrepreneurialism? Tom's curiosity on these matters, his available time and resources, and the steady flow of people asking for his help, all came together in the early

1990s and were the foundation of what became his books, his personal and organizational coaching program, and the ongoing series of Eagle Summits.

"One idea, well executed, can change your life forever."

I don't know how many times I've heard him say this, but Tom just said it again. He can seem like a broken record, but he's not shy about repeating the timeless philosophies that he so passionately believes in.

"Tell me more," I asked Tom.

"The key, Brett, is execution. There are millions of ideas out there, but very few people have the discipline, focus, and persistence to execute the idea. And you don't sit around waiting for the idea," he followed. "Be a learner, be a reader, study other people, especially those further up the spiral staircase of life. You know people are up there, people you admire because of their values, what they've done in their life. Reach out and meet these people, and ask them to help you," he continued.

Reflecting back on my own life, I started to ponder on what "one idea" I had executed well that changed my life forever. Sure, I had my mid-life awakening to the fact that I was on the wrong track in my corporate career, and I changed course. Being an entrepreneur was the right path for me, no doubt, and I was proud of the success I saw in those first few years. But what was my "one idea?"

2007, 2008, 2009, now 2010—the recruiting business was surviving despite the overall economy and the many changes that had taken place in my personal life. After three moves, divorce, and now running my business from my bedroom in the apartment I was sharing with my mother, it was amazing to some that I was still in business. Somehow, through sheer grit and determination, we not only survived, but we remained in the top 10 percent of SRA offices globally. Because of this track record, I was asked to teach new owners of the SRA system a class on how to get started in the recruiting profession, and was also elected to the board of the SRA Owners Association. I enjoyed these activities and observed the growth that was taking place for me personally and professionally. Something, however, was still nagging at me, and I couldn't quite pinpoint the problem.

I had just finished giving a presentation at the SRA spring conference, which was held in Dallas this year. I've given this presentation now for three consecutive years, and the main point of the presentation is how to go about marketing for recruiting projects and what to do to improve upon the closing percentage. In our firm, which was made up of predominantly contingency-type searches, we only get paid if and when a person is hired. My closing rate had now improved to about 25 percent, meaning that we made our money on only one out of four projects that we started.

Even though I was seeing steady improvement in the closing rate on our searches, I was unhappy. People could see that in my demeanor during my presentation, and at a break, one of the other franchise owners asked me what was wrong. I told him that even though I was happy with the improvement, I wanted to move our closing rate much, much higher. I knew the only way to do this was to move from contingency search into retained search. I had no idea how to go about obtaining retained search projects, and was fearful of losing my existing clients, of which I only had a handful, if I tried to convert them to a retained model.

Overhearing my conversation, another franchise owner interrupted, "Brett, you need to go to Sandler Sales Training."

At the coffee break I went into another room and sat down. Reflecting on what was just said to me, I realized that there was a part of me that needed to change. In spite of my overall success as a recruiting business owner, I was, in fact, not a great salesperson. A great salesperson would know what to do to go out and win retained search assignments. A great salesperson would not be afraid of having conversations with existing clients to potentially convert them to a new model. A great salesperson would not be afraid of sales training. I have now heard, over a four year period, three different people tell me that I needed Sandler Sales Training. I'm clearly a slow learner, but this time, I heard the suggestion loud and clear.

Returning home to Durham, I immediately sought out a local Sander Sales Training office, met with the sales trainer, and signed up for the one year program called "President's Club." Meeting weekly with other business owners who were also part of the program, I found the Sandler Sales Training program to be exactly what I needed. I never missed a meeting, and always did my homework, preparing well in advance for each class.

I reluctantly learned that I had a lot of "head trash" buried deep within my psyche with respect to the sales process. I learned that the little boy in me was unconsciously taught to think of sales as a dirty profession, and that talking about money was somehow evil. How in the world can you be good at sales if you are evil when talking about money? Through honest self-reflection, I also realized that part of me was secretly afraid of success.

For two years I was a regular, weekly participant in the Sandler Sales Training program. That experience completely transformed my mental approach to sales, as well as my tactical sales process. Today, our recruiting business is predominantly made up of retained search projects, our closing rate is approaching 80 percent, and most of the work we do is at the senior leadership level. As a company, our satisfaction with our work is much higher, and our clients tend to be business partners, calling upon us over and over for support on new recruiting needs. We have turned our business from a vendor/transactional relationship to a trusted advisor partnership, where the true value of what we deliver is understood by all. None of this would have happened without the transformation that took place in my approach to sales as a result of Sandler Sales Training.

One idea, well executed, that changed my life forever? Got it! That "one idea" was humbly accepting the fact that I desperately needed sales training, and making the financial and time investment to go out and get it. The results were amazing, and transformed the nature of my business and my career. To this date, I continue to read and study the sales profession, knowing that I can always grow and improve in this very important part of my life.

With the Sandler Sales Training example, I was the knucklehead who resisted the recommendations made by several different people over several years. Shame on me. In Tom's RE/MAX example, he was primed and ready to go when Howard suggested he quit his job at the University of Missouri and go with a commission-only scheme to sell RE/MAX franchises in rural Georgia.

The inspiration and the sources for ideas are endless. Some examples that come to mind are:

- Tom Hill's idea back in 1998 to invite 12 people

for a weekend retreat was a new idea, very well-executed. This unusual gathering was the first of what would eventually be 47 and counting Eagle Summits held three times per year in locations all across North America.

- My choice to quit my job at AFL, and to buy and operate my SRA Executive Search franchise was an idea that changed my life forever.
- My idea to create a life coaching and organizational consulting business has changed my life forever.
- Deciding to write this book has changed my life forever.

The key to success for each of these initiatives, however, is execution. Any idea, without execution, is worthless. Most ideas fail because of poor execution.

So how does one come across new ideas? Below are some suggestions:

Be a reader, be a learner. Learning to love to read has been the biggest transformation in my life in the past seven years. Previously a very slow reader, I used the EyeQ program to move my reading speed from 250 words per minute to now over 1000 words per minute, without losing comprehension.

> If you read one book per week, you'll be in the top one percent of adults in America.

Replacing time-wasting activities like watching television with intentionally reading good books is priceless in leading toward personal growth. Reading faster makes the process much more enjoyable. I like to track the books I read, and I use the free online program called Shelfari to keep track of my virtual bookshelf. I invite you to join as well and connect with me to share our reading lists. If you read one book per week, you'll be in the top one percent of adults in America. Be careful, as 85 percent of the books available aren't worth reading. Identify your priorities in life, and commit to reading and learning as much as you can about each of your priorities. There is no stronger commitment that you can make to your authentic personal growth.

Be a networker. I used to be very shy. Meeting new people was extremely uncomfortable. I learned to change this, just like I learned to be a better salesperson. As Tom Hill has taught me,

"Success leaves clues."

If I'm honestly committed to success, to personal growth, then I should learn from those ahead of me on the same path. Tom likes to use the symbolism of looking up a spiral staircase. Pretend that the people who are further up the staircase are those who have achieved greater success in your priority areas of life. It shouldn't just be about financial success, but should be about all areas in your life. As you look up this hypothetical staircase, for which you cannot see all the way to the top, you can see the shoes of some people—you know they are up there, and they have a lot they can share with you. Make a conscious effort to find out who these people are, and connect with them. People love to help other people, especially people who are trying to learn and grow. There are hundreds of books written on techniques for networking, so as Tom has said to me several times, "No excuses, my friend."

> You become the average of the ten adults you spend the most time with.

Be intentional about who you spend time with. This was a wakeup call for me. I found myself spending most of my spare time with the people I worked with, with my neighbors, and with old friends. I was not selective about who I spent time with, and quite frankly thought that if I were to be, I'd be rude. I've since learned to respect the impact that other people have on my life. As Jim Rohn says, "You become the average of the ten adults you spend the most time with." I quickly realized that I didn't want to become the average of the folks I was spending time with, so I went about changing my crowd. Benji Kelley, senior pastor at our church, puts in a different context, saying that we all have an obligation to be very selective about whom we let into our "core." Our core is made up of the folks that have the most influence on the trajectory of our lives. We should love everyone, but not let everyone in our core. This, unfortunately but true, often includes family members. It is not selfish to be focused on your own growth as it relates to your very carefully picked out priorities. It is healthy to do so, and as you grow, you will be even more generous and be able to help other people.

Create or be part of a mastermind group. As Napoleon Hill describes in his best-selling book, *Think and Grow Rich*, a mastermind group is an incredible way to solve problems and facilitate growth among peers. The concept of getting a group of people together to confidentially discuss and help each other with professional and sometimes personal issues goes back thousands of years, and was popularized by Benjamin Franklin and later Napoleon Hill. In our technology-crazy world, it is easy to avoid the face-to-face interaction required by a genuine mastermind group, but the magic that typically takes place in a well-organized mastermind group cannot happen without physically being together on a regular, frequent basis. *Think and Grow Rich* is the ultimate guide for setting up a mastermind group.

Chapter Ten: Goal Setting and the G-Curve

I've been dreading writing this chapter. It is super hard to make a chapter on goal-setting somehow interesting for the reader. While I'm a huge believer in the power of setting goals, and I've seen the phenomenal impact this practice has had on my own life, I almost hate reading anything written about setting goals. I hope you'll bear with me.

Before I reconnected with Tom Hill and started with his coaching program, I did not set goals for my life. I went about my days just doing whatever I was doing, and generally doing pretty well. Starting as a young child, through programming provided primarily by my parents, my grandmother, and teachers at school, I set about living my life.

Young childhood, elementary school, junior high school, high school, college, graduation, a job, marriage, children, MBA, credit cards, mortgage, car payments, 401(k), life insurance, health insurance, car insurance, tuition, church, family, friends, vacations, golf, eventually retirement, grandchildren, and death. I'm sure I missed a few things, but hit the big items. I'm sure for many people, this is their life, and is a wonderful life.

What it was for me was back to autopilot. I chose the wrong college degree. I chose the wrong career. I had a great family, but the marriage ended up not working. I spent two decades in my adult working life before I realized I was on the wrong path. Luckily I woke up before it was too late, and I made some major changes.

Leaving the corporate world behind, where structure was everywhere and all of my working goals were set for me, I felt both wonderful about my new freedom, yet strangely uncomfortable. Going to my new office, in the business that I owned, where I could do as little or as much as I wanted, felt strange. I knew I had a strong work ethic, so I wasn't concerned that I'd be a slacker. What I felt missing was a way to consolidate all of the thousands of different things I could be doing into a set of the most important, most critical, and what I thought, most urgent. I found that I was wrong about the urgent part.

Reading the *Seven Habits of Highly Effective People* by Steven Covey, I learned that as a business owner, I should prioritize those items that are the most important and not the most urgent. Urgent are things like emails, phone calls, unexpected problems and the nagging firefighting that strips away any real progress. Important are things like planning, creating new content, thinking of new strategies, developing new client relationships, and hiring the right people.

I learned with Tom Hill's help that I should set goals on the six priority areas of my life, and specifically within the business I should set goals on the macro-areas of importance that I wanted to drive within the firm.

Tom is a huge proponent of written goals. Several studies have shown that people who write down their goals, each and every day, and carry their goals with them, are much more likely to achieve their goals than people who don't write them down. I've taken this advice to heart, and have created my habit of writing down my goals on a 3x5 index card, each and every day. I've been doing this for five years, and I'll feel somewhat naked if I leave the house without them. At a minimum, I'm convinced that the process of writing down my goals each day is a way to program my subconscious mind to get to work to finding solutions or otherwise helping with the achievement of my goals.

Tom recommends that his coaching clients utilize the SMART goal setting process. By SMART, he is referring to goals in that they should be:

S — Specific
M — Measurable
A — Action-oriented
R — Realistic
T — Time-sensitive

As I mentioned earlier in this book, I like to use a color-coded Excel sheet to track my progress on my goals. Other people use other methods. It doesn't matter how they are tracked, but what is important is that they are top of mind every day, and that there is regular action taken to achieve them.

> "What gets measured gets done."

It is important to know the difference between "process goals" and "results goals." A process goal is a goal related to how or what you will do, the action that you will take. These goals are activities that are completely within your control. A "results goal" or an "outcome goal" is a measurement of the result of your actions, or of your process.

For example, a process goal could be, "I will make twenty sales calls every work day." Doing this, or not doing this, is completely up to you, and within your control. A results goal could be, "I will close new recruiting deals worth fifty thousand dollars per month."

Now, there's nothing wrong with having aspirations for a certain level of results, but since these results are not completely within your control, it is better to prioritize your goal setting efforts on those process-related goals with which you have complete control.

Dr. Jason Selk is a high performance coach for several world-class athletes, and the St. Louis Cardinals baseball team. Jason is also an expert within the Arête coaching program. In his video on process goals, Jason shares that when he coaches a professional baseball player to improve his batting performance, the entire focus is on the swing, on the stance, on the fundamentals and on practice. There is no focus on the outcome. It is much better for a batter to arrive at the plate thinking to himself, "Correct stance, focus on the ball, smooth swing, stay relaxed," versus arriving at the plate thinking, "I've got to get a hit, I've got to get a hit, I simply have to get a hit." It's obvious which approach will work better, and which approach will improve his batting percentage.

The same type of thinking should apply to intelligently setting goals for any area in life or at work.

Here are some other examples, following my six priority areas of life:

Spiritual: Instead of saying, "I must become more spiritual," one could change this to say, "I will pray each morning."

Physical: Instead of saying, "I will lose twenty pounds," one could write, "I will cut out fried foods and run twenty miles each week."

Relationships: Instead of saying, "I will be a better husband," a better goal is to state, "I will take my wife on a date once per week, and will leave my cell phone at home." (I recommend you try this, by the way. She will love it!)

Emotional: Instead of saying, "I will worry less," you could state, "I will meditate ten minutes each weekday morning."

Intellectual/Professional: Instead of saying, "I will get a promotion this year," you could state, "I will volunteer for an extra project once per quarter."

Financial: Instead of saying, "My stock portfolio will be worth one million dollars by year end," you could change this to say, "I will invest one hundred dollars per week into my savings account."

Having "results-related" objectives are fine, but don't confuse these with process goals, and make sure that your process goals are well thought out, are clearly in front of you, and are ready to be approached each and every day.

The idea with this type of goal setting is partially to develop new habits, and also to get specific work done so you can grow in that area in your life. And this shouldn't all be work. It is perfectly fine to have process-related goals around things you enjoy in life. My example of a relationship goal is to take my wife out on a weekly basis. I love doing this, so there's no sacrifice here.

If one of your objectives is to get better at golf, then write it down. However, instead of saying your goal is to reduce your handicap to a seven, a better process goal would be to say that you will practice your swing two hours per week, and practice putting one hour per week. If you actually did this, you can guarantee that you would reduce your handicap. An even better goal would be to hire a golf coach and set goals on how much you would work with him or her.

Another suggestion is to make all of your goals or objectives positive statements. For example, instead of saying, "I will not spend more than twenty dollars on fast food each week," it would be better to say, "I will eat healthy foods whenever I have that option."

Instead of saying, "I'm not going to catch a cold this year," it is better to say, "I will be completely healthy this winter."

There's a part of our subconscious that can't differentiate between the words won't, not, can't, etc. When you say, "I won't catch a cold," part of your brain only hears the words "I catch a cold." If you say to yourself, "I don't want to get in debt," there's a part of your brain that hears, "I want to get in debt." Dr. Wayne Dyer, who is one of my all-time favorite authors, puts it this way: The good news—whatever you really, really, really, really want, you will get. The bad news—whatever you really, really, really, really don't want, you will also get.

I think you get it. I urge you to try it. It works, believe me.

A question I hear all the time is, "How often should I adjust my goals, and how do I find the discipline to make them stick?"

On the discipline question, the first answer is to make sure that your goals are in alignment with your priority areas of life. You must be absolutely clear on your priorities, without fuzziness, before any type of goal setting will work. We all know what happens at year end with respect to New Year's resolutions. People get all worked up about changes they want to make for the coming year, and the fitness centers make a boatload of money on people who buy memberships and then quit coming after the second week in January. I chuckle as I see this phenomenon repeat itself every year without fail at my fitness center.

Why does this happen? It is simple. The people who set these New Year's resolutions about their weight, exercise, etc. have not honestly set their physical health as a key priority in their life. They are not bad people, and they are in good company, as most Americans have not set their own physical health as a priority. Our culture makes this extremely difficult to do, and therefore honest goal setting, focusing on activity as opposed to results measurements, is key.

In addition to making sure that goals are set in alignment with life's priorities, it is also important that goals are set with the right timeframe involved. Tom Hill is an expert on this subject, and he has studied hundreds of people as he developed his goal setting program.

A key part of Tom's life coaching approach is a unique concept called the G-Curve. The G-Curve, or also called the Growth Curve, is an adaptation of Moore's Law, first published in 1965 by Gordon Moore. Gordon Moore was the cofounder of Intel, the company which first produced the modern microprocessor. Moore's Law predicted that the speed of an integrated circuit, otherwise known as a computer chip, would double every 18 months. Furthermore, the price would go down fifty percent. To date, Moore's Law has been remarkably accurate, even though technologies not remotely considered back in 1965 are now commonplace.

As Tom Hill studied the lives of successful people, and as he diagnosed many of the significant events that took place in his own life, as well as the lives of people he coached, he recognized that Moore's Law, or the G-Curve, applies as well to personal growth. Tom saw that tipping points, or otherwise referred to as breakthrough moments in personal or professional growth, often take place at or near the 18 month time frame. These tipping points can sometimes propel a person to a significantly higher level of performance or capacity.

This 18 month phenomenon for personal growth is certainly not scientific, and can't be proven, but has been observed over and over. There is something magical about the number 18 in the Jewish religion, and Jesus's ministry on earth lasted about two G-curves, or 36 months. With his coaching clients, Tom suggests that goals be set, and written in six-year, three-year, 18-month and 90-day increments. Six years is the equivalent of four distinct G-curves, and is enough time to significantly transform one's life. Tom believes that it takes 18 months, or one G-curve, to permanently eliminate a bad habit, and also to create a new habit. In Tom's experience, most people will give up on a new initiative, especially one requiring breaking a bad habit, way before they reach the 18 month mark. For most new goals, the student will see good progress for the first several weeks and maybe even months. Then somewhere along the way progress will slow and reach a plateau. This is often at around the one-year mark.

For many people, this is the point at which they will simply give up. Some people will continue on their journey, and start to see a dip in their performance. This dip is similar to the phenomenon described in Seth Godin's fantastic book by the same title, *The Dip*.

According to Godin, one of three options will take place upon encountering a dip:

1. You will give up.
2. You are on the wrong path, you recognize it, and you turn around and go back. This is referred to as a cul-de-sac.
3. You are on the right path, you recognize that you are simply in a dip, in a slump, you lean into it as if you were on a ski slope, and then rise back up to an even higher point than when you started.

Path number three described by Seth Godin is typical in Tom's observations of successful people over the years that he has been coaching. Tom has seen, over and over, where a huge breakthrough will take place, sometimes exactly on the date of the 18 month mark, propelling the coaching client to much higher levels.

The image below illustrates the G-Curve concept:

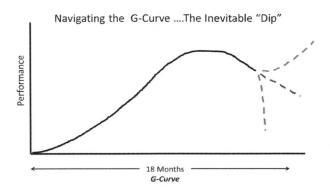

Navigating the G-Curve ....The Inevitable "Dip"

When Tom and Betty first listened to the worn-out Jim Rohn tapes, Tom was a frustrated administrator within the university system. Eighteen months later, they met with Howard and decided to embark upon the RE/MAX journey.

When Tom and Betty first set out on their journey to sell RE/MAX franchises in South Georgia, they had nothing but $36,000, a truck and travel trailer, their clothes, and a dream. Eighteen months later, one G-Curve later, they owned the rights to RE/MAX in six states.

The stories are fascinating, and go on and on. I have several in my own life, but that is not the point I want to make. The most important part of the G-Curve concept is to set goals, or objectives if that makes more sense, for 18-month time horizons. Then, break these objectives into 90-day process goals, and monitor your performance and progress daily. By doing this, and by staying on the path, you will be putting the odds in your favor, and will most likely achieve the goals that you have set. Sticking to it, over the long run, or in this case, for 18 months, is the magic formula for achieving your dreams.

Chapter Eleven: The Journey Continues

I'm not superstitious, and if I were, I'd be looking behind my back. Things in my life have gone incredibly well, too well, so there must be a big old dose of bad news coming my way. Like I said, I'm not superstitious, so I'll drop this passing thought.

I do know that life can be bumpy, or crunchy as I like to put it, and there's no free pass for anyone from life's hurts and pains. I think I have developed resiliency from which to get through life's challenges, and I'm not afraid to tackle the tough stuff.

Life in Durham, North Carolina, has unfolded for me in ways that I could only dream. Becoming increasingly involved at newhope church, Kim and I are now regular volunteers as greeters, we lead a Wednesday night small group at a friend's house, volunteer at the Durham Rescue Mission, and we tithe. Many of our best friends are people we met at newhope church, and our social circle is expanding quickly.

When I lived in Michigan, and through encouragement from Tom as we focused on the "Relationships" part of my life, he suggested that I look for non-profit organizations on which to serve, preferably on their boards. Upon moving to Durham, I restarted this initiative, and I'm now serving on the Board of Directors of two great organizations, The

Arc of the Triangle, which provides support for people with intellectual and developmental disabilities, and the Lung Transplant Foundation, which is raising funds to drive research to find a cure for chronic lung transplant rejection. While the work I do for both of these boards often conflicts with the time I can devote to my business, I know it is the right thing to do. I'm growing on a professional level, I am meeting some wonderful people, and it's all part of my plan to grow as a person and to make a positive difference in the world.

My recruiting company has continued to grow, and we have successfully made the transition to a retained model. Despite my prolonged resistance to the repeated recommendations, my immersion into Sandler Sales Training was central to this transition, and probably saved the company from ruin. In 2013 I added a new partner to the firm, Gary Scypta, based in Plymouth, Michigan, who brought with him a decade of experience in senior level retained search. In 2014 I added a partnership with Carlos Kingwergs, an experienced recruiter with offices in Houston, Texas, and Mexico City. Given this growth, and the fact that we now have offices in Durham, Louisville, Colorado Springs, Detroit, Houston and Mexico City—I renamed the recruiting company Sanford Rose Associates–Blair Leadership Group.

Continuing to be in the top 10 percent of offices in the global SRA network, I was proud to receive awards at the annual conferences. At the conference in San Diego in March 2014, with Kim in the audience, I was surprised to be awarded the "Corporate Mystic" award. I later learned that this award was created to recognize the office owner who went above and beyond his/her own self interests in support of others.

Public speaking was starting to become a bigger part of my life, with numerous opportunities coming my way. Continuing on the previous times I had formally taught new office owners how to get started with their recruiting companies, I was asked to videotape a presentation for SRA training company called Next Level Exchange. Flying to Dallas to use their video studio and green screen, I had my first experience speaking into a camera with a teleprompter. It was cool, and whet my appetite to do more presentations via video technology.

I gave a presentation in Novi, Michigan, called *The Top Ten Tactics to Get the Right People on the Bus*, and also gave a speech, *The World Needs You to be You*, which was recorded as part of the Undivided 36x36 event in St. Louis in September 2013. Working with Curt Steinhorst as my speech coach, I developed and later delivered a speech at the Raleigh Eagle Summit in October 2014, titled *The Five Tactics to Win the War for Talent*.

Kim and I have attended several Eagle Summits, and I was energized when I heard that Dr. Roger Hall was leading a program to train additional life coaches, called High Performance Advisors, in the coming months. I immediately signed up for the class, and over a one-year period, with several three-day live sessions in St. Louis as well as monthly video calls, I, along with five other Hill's Angels, went through the rigorous training and I ultimately received my certification as an HPA. Going through this class, which I absolutely loved, reinforced my conviction that my real calling in life is in helping other people, and specifically through life coaching.

Speaking of coaching, my monthly coaching call with Tom Hill is coming up next week. As with each of my prior coaching calls, I am expected to provide an email update on what's been going on in my life, and to refresh my goals. It is time for me to be thinking about my next G-Curve, but before doing that, I probably should assess my current level of balance. By the way, I don't believe that anyone should ever rank themselves as a perfect ten on any category. There is always room for growth. Here we go:

Spiritual: I give myself a nine. I'm reading from *The Message* translation of the Bible every morning. I'm meditating every day for at least 10 minutes. Kim and I are super-active at newhope church, including leading a Life Group. In additional to tithing, we just committed a great deal of money for the three-year capital campaign. I quietly pray every morning when I wake, and Kim and I pray regularly before meals. Most importantly, I feel peace in my soul.

Physical: Nine. I just finished the Savannah Half Marathon in under two hours, with no injuries and my body felt great. I've taken the APO-E gene test from Pam McDonald's company, author of *The Perfect Gene Diet*, and I've modified my diet to her suggestions. I'm looking forward to getting my blood tests and seeing what has happened to my cholesterol levels. I'm lifting weights at the fitness center twice per week. Overall, I feel great!

Relationships: Eight. My marriage with Kim is a ten plus! I couldn't be happier and she is the blessing of my world. I crave a close relationship with all three of my adult children, and for this, I commit to making a conscious effort. My professional relationships are great and I'm continuing to meet new people, in North Carolina and elsewhere, partially through connections made via Tom Hill and through the Eagle Summits.

Emotional: Eight. Overall great here. I do have moments of guilt and regret for the divorce and the pain that I caused. I continue to regularly read books that build upon my emotional health. I just finished *The Obstacle is the Way* by Ryan Holiday, which is fantastic.

Intellectual/Professional: Nine. I'm thrilled with how things are going with my recruiting business, and am excited about my new plans with the coaching business, Blair Leadership Group. Writing this book has been a significant challenge, and getting it completed and published is a big milestone.

Financial: Seven. I love how Kim and I are absolutely on the same page regarding our finances. With our mortgage being our only debt, we are both committed to staying debt-free. If I could go back in time and recover all the money I flushed away by buying and leasing new cars every couple of years, as well as buying new homes before I sold the previous ones, I would be rich. But thank God I learned some valuable lessons on managing money later in life, primarily from listening to Dave Ramsey. I'll never go back to buying new cars. Credit card debt has never been a problem, but it is one that Kim and I are both committed to keeping out of our lives. I'm still recovering from the costs of the divorce, but making steady progress. I'd also like to level out some of the variability in income from the recruiting business. Our plan is to pay off our mortgage as soon as we can, continue to tithe and give generously to the church and other causes, to travel a lot and visit friends and family, and to save responsibly for our future. Neither one of us have a need or interest in many physical things, we don't have expensive hobbies, other than my Amazon Prime crack habit of buying books. We have a relatively modest lifestyle, and simply want to enjoy each

other, our health, this beautiful planet, family and friends.
A look at my Circle of Life now shows:

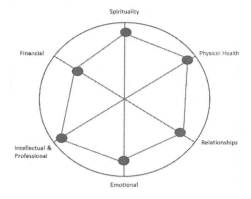

"This stuff works."

Tom Hill often says this about the whole process of goal setting and life coaching—this stuff works. I'm sure seeing it play out in my life, and couldn't be more thrilled.

* * *

I'm feeling anxious. Having not spoken to her for over three years, I'm not sure how this will go. Alimony payments being written every month, I recently set these up on auto-payment out of my checking account so I wouldn't have to physically write the check each time. It just brought back too many sad memories.

Dana and Lee are getting married this weekend in Spring Hill, Tennessee. Dana met her fiancé while in college at Auburn. They were both marketing majors, and Lee, a big old bear of a young man, actually grew up in the small town of Auburn, Alabama. A great guy, gentle and with a huge heart, we were all thrilled when we learned about their engagement. Dana and Lee were now living together out in Colorado Springs, Colorado, near her brother Patrick. Patrick had moved out there a couple of years earlier to go to college at the University of Colorado—Colorado Springs. Dana and Lee fell in love with the town and that part of the country, so they packed up and moved from Franklin, Tennessee. I was proud of them both for taking that brave, independent step.

The wedding will be the first time that I will have seen Carol, her mother, and many other friends and previous family. Also, it will be the first time that any of these folks, other than my three kids and Joan and Joey, Carol's sister and brother-in-law, will have met Kim. Kim was a real trooper about it all, and didn't show any anxiety as the big date came closer. I was sure anxious, not knowing how Carol would react to seeing me or Kim. We certainly hadn't left things on a friendly basis when we divorced back in 2009.

The wedding was on a Saturday afternoon. On the Friday before, a bridesmaid's lunch was arranged for all the ladies, and Kim was invited. She didn't hesitate to accept the invitation, and drove to the luncheon, along with my mom, Gretchen, my brother's wife, and Bailey, my nephew's wife. They were one of the first to arrive at the restaurant, and Kim and Carol were soon introduced. Pacing alone in our hotel room after Kim had left, I tried desperately to keep my mind on other things. I couldn't help but watch the clock, wondering how things were going. Anxiety was building with each minute. My cell phone finally rang, over two hours after they left the hotel. "How'd it go?" I blurted out.

"It went really well," Kim calmly said. "Carol was super sweet and nice to me, and so was her mom. She looked great, and the luncheon was really nice." I exhaled with relief.

The outdoor wedding was beautiful. Eric, Dana's biological father, and I together walked Dana down the aisle. The wedding was followed by a reception held on the grounds of the Civil War-era plantation house where the ceremony took place. Having rained the entire day before, the clouds parted and the sun shone on the ceremony as if the weather was perfectly scripted. Dana has never been more radiant and beautiful, and the event went off without a hitch. Carol and I had a couple of pleasant moments of light chit chat alone, and kept our comments to how beautiful Dana and Lee both were, and how happy we were that they were together. Carol did not have a date at the wedding, and spent most of her time either with her mother, or with other family and friends. I hugged Carol goodbye as Kim and I left for our hotel at the end of the reception.

Although the monthly alimony expenses were still very much a part of my reality, I felt a huge sense of relief after the wedding was over. I didn't realize how much anxiety was building inside of me with respect to seeing Carol again. Kim was fantastic throughout the entire weekend, and she made a number of new friends. I don't know why I would expect anything else, and I was proud to be her husband.

Back in Durham and life as normal. The leaves are changing colors and beginning to fall. The backyard in our new home in Durham is heavily wooded, and leaves are falling on the grassy area faster than I can rake them up. I hate doing yard work, so I put this off as much as I can.

Kim was married before to a great guy named Dan. Dan fought depression for much of his adult life, and Kim knew this when they married. He got counseling, was on medication, and was able to manage things well, for most of the time. Dan took his own life one afternoon in their home. Kim was devastated, but was held up by the love of her friends, her church family, as well as the depression support group she had been part of in Jacksonville Beach. Kim soon moved to a small condominium a few miles away, and rented out the house where she and Dan had previously lived. For several years, Kim tried to get on with her life, focusing on work, church, family and friends. Dating proved to be difficult, and it was hard to leave the shadow of being a young widow.

Kim worked in the marketing department at Blue Cross and Blue Shield of Florida. She loved her job there, but was concerned about her future as layoffs were being announced as part of a restructuring. She took this as a clue that she may want to start looking outside the company for another job. Kim considered moving to North Carolina to be closer to her sister, Sharon, who lived in Cary, and who, along with her husband Bo, had recently adopted a little girl. Applying for a position online, Kim was hired by Blue Cross and Blue Shield of North Carolina to work in their marketing department. She took this job, moved to a small apartment, and courageously began the next phase of her life. It was just under a year later when I met Kim through the magic of eHarmony.

Kim remained close with Dan's brother and his family, who live in Maryland. Joe and his wife, Kim, have two daughters, Maddie and Catie, who love Kim for the special aunt that she is. The entire family readily accepted me into their lives, and I view Maddie and Catie as my nieces as well.

Maddie, a star volleyball player in high school, had accepted a scholarship to play volleyball for Mars Hill College near Asheville, North Carolina. Mars Hill had a volleyball match at a small college about two hours away from where we live in Durham, and we decided we would drive there one Friday night to watch Maddie play.

Kim left work early that Friday, and we drove the one hundred miles to the school's campus. Finding the gymnasium and a place to park, we were thrilled when we saw Maddie warming up on the gym floor as we walked in. Big bear hugs were shared, and Kim and I settled in on the hard bleachers to watch the three matches.

One hour into the match, my cell phone rang, but it was too loud in the gymnasium to take the call. I could see that it was Dana calling, but I let it go to voice mail. My guess was she was calling to thank Kim and I for the wedding gift, which was left at the wedding a few weeks earlier. Twenty minutes later my cell phone rang again, and this time it was a call from Joan, Carol's sister. I let this go to voice mail as well. I wasn't too concerned, as Joan and I are unusually close, given what happened to my marriage with her sister, and we talk from time to time. I told Kim about both calls, and we exchanged looks of concern. After the three matches were over, we hugged Maddie, and walked back to my car in the chilly night.

"You should call them back," Kim said as we got into the car. "Why don't you do it before we get going?" Nervously I hit redial on the message from Joan, and the call went directly to her voice mail. I left a brief message, trying to sound chipper, and then went on to call Dana. Dana answered the phone, and I could tell that she had been crying. "Hi, Dana, it's Pop. What's wrong?"

"It's Mom. She's dead."

"Oh my God. I'm so sorry. What happened?"

"I don't know, Pop. They found her in her barn. She had been shot," Dana sobbed.

"Oh my God, Oh my God, I'm so very, very sorry." I looked over at Kim, and whispered that Carol was dead, and that she had been shot. Kim looked away.

My head was spinning with a thousand questions, but I knew that Dana didn't need to be the one to hear all that. For some reason, I immediately suspected suicide. I had obviously known Carol for a long, long time, and although she had never threatened suicide, and had never gone to counseling for depression, I knew that she had emotional challenges. Thank God we had never owned a gun when we were married. I heard that Carol had bought a shotgun after her house in Christiana was burglarized several years prior.

"Pop, they don't know if one of her crazy old boyfriends did it, or what."

"Dana, I love you. I'm so very, very sorry. How did you find out?"

"Joan called and told me," she replied.

I could see Joan was now calling back on my cell phone. "Dana, Joan is calling me now. Let me talk to her, and I'll give you a call back."

Joan confirmed the details, and shared that it was not clear whether the gunshot was self-inflicted. She told me that all three kids had been notified, and I thanked her for letting me know, and that I would call Patrick and Ellen to check on them.

The rest of the night, and the rest of the weekend was a blur. Kim was amazingly resilient and held me up through the emotional roller coaster ride that I was going through. It was suicide, and notes were found that exposed the depth of Carol's anguish over the previous years. The kids were in shock, as well as Carol's mother and other family members. I was deeply saddened, replaying in my mind the highs and lows of twenty years of marriage to this sweet lady. I felt so badly for all three kids, and wished there was more I could do to help them.

The funeral was held five days later on a cold, windy, gray

day in middle Tennessee. It was the saddest thing I've ever been part of. All three kids were brave and held each other up through the grueling weekend. I stayed in the background as it felt like it was the best thing I could do, but I was also there for each of the kids as much as they needed me. Kim did the smart thing and stayed back in Durham.

When I shared the news with Pastor Benji, he immediately responded that this was part of why God put Kim and I together. Knowing that Kim too had experienced the loss of her husband to suicide, Benji had the foresight to make this comment. This somehow comforted me, and I so deeply appreciated the support and wisdom that Kim shared, as I tried to put the pieces back together and somehow make sense of this terrible tragedy.

"Life can get crunchy."

That's what I say to my kids and what I say to myself. It is hard growing up, and it is hard being a grown-up. Our challenge is to see the beauty in life, the beauty in our world, the beauty in each other, in spite of the terrible things that can and will happen along the way. I'm proud of my three children; I love them unconditionally and wish each of them a life full of love and promise, health and hope.

Chapter Twelve: The Best is Yet to Come

"If you could wave your magic wand, and if you didn't have to make money, what would you do?" Tom asked during our very first coaching call back in 2007.

"Wow, I've never considered that. How could that ever happen?" I replied.

"It can happen, and it probably will," was his immediate response. I soon learned that this is exactly what happened to Tom and Betty after they sold their RE/MAX businesses. With time and money on his hands, Tom shifted his priorities to helping other people.

Helping other people has always been my passion. As far back as I can remember I've always enjoyed helping people. I remember helping the old ladies at the nursing home when I was in Boy Scouts, and loved helping people when I worked at Blue Springs Bank. I loved my job at the Dairy Queen, as it was all about dealing with people. Somehow along the way, I got totally derailed, and decided to choose engineering as my career. Big mistake number one! I honestly don't know how or why I got so confused. I let money and a regular paycheck obscure my passions.

Twenty years later, I left that big mistake, and started my recruiting business. Thank God I did, and I've loved almost every minute of it.

I'm still saying, every morning when I wake up, that same old Eagle Scout Prayer, but now as I say it, I also thank God for making that prayer come true.

"Dear God. Please forgive me of my sins. Please help me to become a better person. Please help me to be strong and happy."

I now know that, through Christ, my sins have been forgiven. I know that each day I am becoming a better person, and I am strong and happy. Thank you, God!

"Dear God, please bless me. Bless me in ways I can't imagine. It is through your blessings to me that I can be able to help and bless other people.

Please add to my territory—by growing my network each and every day. I want to touch and help more and more people.

Please lift me up as you ask me to do big things—things that I have never done before."

…Wow! This prayer has come true in huge ways. I am blessed beyond measure, and I don't ever want to take that for granted. I am reaching and helping more and more people, each and every day, whether through my recruiting business, through my coaching business, through the church, non-profit boards, volunteer activities, and just in traveling and making friends around the world. Learning to be a better husband, a better father, a better salesman, a better business person, a better leader, a life coach, a public speaker, and now—in writing and publishing this book, God, you have lifted me up in ways that I could never have imagined. Thank you, God!

"Please keep me from evil— from sin."

I trust that God will continue to have my back. Knowing that personal discipline is a choice, I also recognize that I am a human being with human tendencies and weaknesses, and pray that God will help me stay within the guardrails of a decent, righteous life.

"Dear God—thank you. Thank you for all of my countless blessings. I love you. Amen."

What would I do if I could wave my magic wand, and do anything I wanted? The answer is clear and simple—I would help other people. To be more specific, I would coach people. I would coach people on the principles and techniques that Tom Hill and others have taught me. I would help people get unstuck, help them grow, help them find balance, and help them achieve their own unique version of their exceptional lives.

This is my passion, this is my gift, and this is my business. Through the Blair Leadership Group, a coaching and consulting business running in parallel to my recruiting company, Sanford Rose Associates–Blair Leadership Group, I am in a position to turn my passion of helping more people into a reality.

I've been coaching people, formally and informally, for several years. Now it is time to take it to another level.

Here's what I believe:

- I believe that we each have unique God-given gifts. We have strengths, talents, passions, and purpose, and it is our obligation to recognize and maximize those gifts.

- I believe that a life that is intentionally designed and managed to be well-balanced and growing is the best kind of life, and is the blueprint for personal and professional success and happiness.

- I believe that people should commit to growth for their lifetimes, literally. I think the word "retire" should be retired—to the trash can. Living a life of working forty-plus years in jobs you hate, just to save some money and then one day retire and die—that is not a formula for an exceptional life.

- I believe that the world in which we live is getting better, not worse. I believe that media and the human appetite for bad news are creating the inaccurate illusion that the condition of this world is becoming worse over time.

- I believe that the best, for you, for me, for our children, and for the world at large, is yet to come.

May God bless you and yours, now and forever.

Thank you for reading this, my first book. As a young child, I dreamed of writing a book. Now I've done it, and I will write many more. I appreciate the effort you have taken to hear my story. I would love to hear your comments, feedback, or your stories. Please take a minute and write me at bblair@blairleadershipgroup.com. I promise to respond, and look forward to hearing from you.

Also, if you are interested in learning more about my coaching, consulting and speaking services, and if you'd like to join our mailing list, please send me an email or check out my website at www.blairleadershipgroup.com.

I wish you a life of meaning, balance, growth, health and happiness!

Thanks,

Brett A. Blair

Principles of an Exceptional Life

- We are all blessed beyond measure.
- The best is yet to come.
- One idea, well executed, can change your life forever.
- One person, attracted to you because of who you have become, can change your life forever.
- Everyone has a moral obligation to be the very best person they can be.
- Everyone has a moral obligation to make a positive difference in the lives of all people they come in contact with.
- We are all spiritual beings, having a short physical experience.
- Determine your life's priorities, and strive for balance in each.
- Write down your goals, and set goals in six-year, three-year, 18-month and 90-day time horizons.
- Understand and apply the principles of the G-Curve.
- Recognize that most people don't get it. Don't let that slow you down.
- You are the average of the 10 adults you spend the most time with. Choose wisely.
- Connect with people further up the spiral staircase. Success leaves clues.

- Personal discipline leads to personal freedom.
- Put the odds in your favor (OIYF).
- Money is attracted by who you have become.
- Money does not change anyone; it just becomes an amplifier of who you already are.
- Understand synchronicity, and be on the lookout for predictable miracles.

About the Author

Brett Blair is a life coach / High Performance Advisor and founder of The Blair Leadership Group, a life and leadership coaching and consulting firm. Brett also founded and leads Sanford Rose Associates–Blair Leadership Group, an executive search company. Prior to establishing his firm in 2007, Brett earned an industrial engineering degree, an MBA, and enjoyed a 25-year corporate career in international business. Brett's passion is helping people, and he has the real-world experience and practical perspectives from which to be able to advise professionals in a variety of industries and during all seasons of life. Brett has a unique perspective on personal growth and happiness, and is recognized for his ability to lead others to maximize their own potential through living a life of purpose, balance and significance. He enjoys coaching people through a transformative process of self-discovery, thought observation, and modification of thinking patterns. Brett is a relentless optimist, has strong faith in God, believes that the world is abundant, beautiful and full of new opportunities, and that each day brings the promise of renewal and a new beginning. Brett lives with his wife, Kim, in Durham, North Carolina.

Brett can be contacted at bblair@blairleadershipgroup.com, and through his website at www.blairleadershipgroup.com.

Acknowledgments

I couldn't have written this book without help. First of all, I give thanks to my incredible wife, Kim Blair, for her steadfast love and support throughout the process of writing this book. As my soulmate, Kim knows me better than anyone, and was instrumental in seeing that my true voice showed up.

The book would not have been possible without Tom Hill, and the incredible impact he has had, and continues to have on my life. I hope that this book somehow honors Tom for the legacy he will leave with me and the countless others that he has touched.

I thank my family for all of their support and the impact they all have had on my life. To my parents, Judy Weyrauch and Tom Blair, I say thank you for raising me to be a strong and resilient man. You both were and continue to be wonderful parents.

To my three children, I love you unconditionally and wish you each long lives of fullness and blessings. Love to Ellen Green, Dana Speed and Patrick Blair.

I received amazing support from my editor and friend, Alice Osborn, who patiently guided me and taught me the power of the Hero's Journey approach to writing a memoir. I look forward to working on many future book projects with Alice.

I give thanks to Gary Baker for encouraging this book, to Dr. Roger Hall for pouring his wisdom and counsel into me as his HPA student, to Al Curtis and Sandi Maki for showing me the path of creative endeavor in business, to Pastor Benji Kelley for promoting my spiritual growth and providing an amazing church home, and to my full team at SRA-Blair Leadership Group for supporting my extra-curricular activities (this book, for one) as we grow our recruiting business.

There are dozens of others that I have failed to mention, but they know who they are, and to them, I say, "Thank You."